Forever Young

HOW TO FEEL, LOOK AND BE MAGNIFICENT AT ANY AGE

Ella Ladon Croney PHD

Forever Young

*How to Feel, Look and
Be Magnificent at Any Age
Ella Ladon Croney*

Copyright Revision © 2020 by Ella Ladon Croney

ISBN 978-0-9797638-1-6

Published by:
Ella Croney Productions

All rights exclusively reserved. No part of this book may be reproduced or translated into any language or utilized in any form or by any means, electronic or mechanical, including photocopying, recording or by any information storage and retrieval system, without permission in writing from the publisher.

DISCLAIMER

The content of this book is informational only. It should not be considered medical advice. The experiences shared by myself and others aged 50 years and beyond are for self-empowerment and self-improvement. Please consult your health practitioner before considering any of these therapies or healing modalities.

— Ella Croney

Edited by Becky Person and Tony Stubbs

Design and layout by Tony Stubbs, www.tjpublish.com

Printed in the United States of America

CONTENTS

Acknowledgments	1
Gratitudes	3
A Different Kind of Beginning	5
Chapter One	7
50 Is Fabulous	7
The Wake-up Call	9
The Search Continues	10
The Past Meets the Present	13
Chapter Two	19
Applied Kinesiology	19
NAET	22
Tea Infusions	25
Menopause – a gift to a new, empowered you	25
Chapter Three	27
Get More Oxygen	27
Ozone Therapy	30
Lymphatic Cleanse	33
Chapter Four	37
Deep Internal Cleansing	37
Coffee Enemas	40
Cleansing Formulas	41
Chapter Five	43
Herbs	43
Herbs from the Kitchen	44
From Mother's Market and Kitchen – Nutrition News:	44
Ginkgo Biloba	45
Essential Oils	45
Vitamins	48
Vitamins for Our Children	49
Sugar Substitutes	51
Colostrum: the Immune System's Best Friend	53
Collagen for Beautiful Skin from the Inside Out	54

Arbonne's Hybrids	55
Cranberry Capsules, Acidophilus and Enzymes	55
Tools for Dealing with COVID-19	55
The Green Revolution – Wheatgrass/Green Drinks	57
Reactions to Herbs	58
The Nervous System	59
Dealing with Arthritis Naturally	61
The Aqua Chi Water Energy System:	62
Therapeutic Footspa - Healing for the entire family.	62
Bone Health	63

Chapter Six	65
Youth and Vitality - Hollywood's Best Kept Secret	65
Brain State Training – Another Best Kept Secret	66
More Brain State Synchronizing – Fun, Fun, Fun!	69
Some More Fun for Brain Harmony	70
Brain Balancing Meditation: New Life	72
Silva Mind Centering Meditation	72
Health Today	73

Chapter Seven	77
Massage Therapy	77
Acupuncture	78
Reiki	79
Mastering Alchemy	80
DNA Healing – Clearing Internal Clutter	81
Theta Healing and Coaching	83
Change Your Encodements, Your DNA, Your Life!	84

Chapter Eight	85
Balancing Your Home with Basic Feng Shui	85
Family Area: Green/Wood (left side middle)	86
Wisdom/Skills/Knowledge Area: Blue Color (front entrance - left side)	87
Helpful People/Travel Area: Gray/Silver (front entrance - right side)	88
Health Area: Yellow (near the center of your home)	89
Creativity and Children Area: White/Metal (right side middle)	90
Relationship Area: Think Pink (back corner - right side)	91
Wealth Area/Show Me the Money, Honey:	93

Color Purple (back wall - left side)	
Career Area: Color Black (front - middle entrance)	95
Fame and Reputation: Color Red (Back middle-wall)	96
Testimonials	97
Balancing Your Life with Spirituality	98
Spirituality: Ho'oponopono	100
Flower Essences	101
Drinking Water and Bath Soaks - Hydrate! Hydrate!	103
Bath Soaks	105
The All American Diet and the Raw Family	106
When Air Travel Hits a Bump in the Road	108
Holistic and Naturopath Doctors	110
Nurturing for Spiritual Balance and Sanity	112
Chapter Nine	115
Deposits of Wealth	115
Healthy Living through Pain	118
Manifesting Before the Secret	119
Abundance	120
A Creative Lifestyle	122
Vallecitos Mountain Ranch	125
Quickies - Here's Your Bonus Page	127
Do's and Don'ts	129
About the Author	131

ACKNOWLEGMENTS

Gifts sometimes come in strange packaging – something that sent me to the Emergency Room one night for a series of tests, and I was told to see my own doctor the next day. That seemingly negative event became one of the greatest gifts of my life. Fed up with conventional methods and not knowing what had happened to me led me to a conventional doctor practicing non-conventional methods to find that I had toxic poisoning from bad air quality in the airplane I had worked on for four days straight.

I want to show my gratitude and appreciation for Dr. Previtera and Dr. Eberle who showed me more ways to cleanse my body of toxins that could eventually have become major hazards to my health.

To all the flight attendants and pilots who I've shared these methods with and the methods they've shared with me to pass on to you, I am grateful.

To my Alaska Airlines family that has created a joyful lifestyle for me in the last 20 years, I am grateful. And I am grateful that the MD80 is no longer a part of the Alaska Airlines fleet.

To so many of my friends who have shared with me vitamins, herbs and formulas that I now share with you. I give thanks to Carolyn, Samantha, Marcia, Zofea, Christina, Rosemary, Rex, Dr. Devi and Mala and Mohan for making this book possible and helping people live healthy lives through their practices.

To my parents, aunts, uncles, and cousins especially Gregory for their belief in me along with my wonderful son, Luron, who has been my creative joy throughout all of his life. To his Dad, Paul, who gifted me with the joy of Motherhood. My intelligent grandson Cortez and his sister, Christina, are blessings.

To my wonderful teachers Marga, Georgia, Richard, Mario and Linda, Carol Dore, Billy Roberts and Daniel who have always been there for my spiritual and emotional growth.

To my friend Becky who assisted me with my Feng Shui articles for a magazine in Orange County and did the first edit of this book.

I am thankful, of course, for my amazing editor and book designer Tony Stubbs, for whose expertise, assistance and friendship I'm grateful.

Thanks for my son and Penny Welton for adding their creativity to this project.

To many others who help bring this from my table to your table, I give thanks.

And to my readers, may you all be blessed with the rich increase of God's almighty good, and stay healthy along the way.

— Ella Ladon Croney

GRATITUDES

> "I slept and dreamt that life was joy,
> I awoke and saw that life was service.
> I acted and behold, Service was Joy."
> — Rabin-dranath-Tagore

I feel grateful and privileged to share this information from a place of true experiences with you. There is no reason why you can't be strong, powerful, healthy and dynamic in the second phase of your life.

The happiness I hope for you must come from within but first, the healthiness must be present. When you don't feel good, it shows on your face, how you walk, how you talk, how you carry yourself and present yourself to the world, and in your attitude about the world around you where you move and have your very being.

You were born to live a passionate life, a joyous life, and yes, as my friend Richard says, "A juicy life."

Where do we go from here? First understand and get a firm grip on where you are, as opposed to where you want to be, and how you want to live the rest of your life.

Use the resources in this book to educate yourself about healthy alternatives and let nothing and no one stop you from feeling and being magnificent.

From my grandmother Nancy Ella Washington: "Sweetie keep your head up, know you're beautiful and just do the best you can."

Peace and Blessings,
Ella Ladon Croney

A DIFFERENT KIND OF BEGINNING

The original version of this book was and still is a book about change. Changing as we age, and discovering that our health is our true wealth. Little did I know ten years later, just how much change would take place in the consciousness of humanity.

The majority of the world's population had no fore-warning that COVID19 would arrive purposely or by accident. Either way, it enforced a change upon us.

The first version of my book in 2010 was written for people over 50 years of age, entering the second half of their lives. I too, am in that stage of my life's journey. It was and still is based upon Natural & Preventive ways to take charge of our health. We can use these different modalities for healing minor & major illnesses, as I shared in the real life stories presented here.

More now than ever before, because of the global pandemic COVID19, the information presented in this book's latest revision will also assist the younger generations and possibly generations to come.

According to The Business Insider, "as of 2020, the U.S. ranks #30 in healthcare and education." That is a huge decline from ranking #6 back in 1990. This tells us all that we cannot afford to leave our education or health in the hands of the government.

Picking up this book is an investment that guarantees that you attract more ways to live a healthy, joyous, and magical life at any age. This is my world, and it can be your world….and we can all live as witnesses to it and share all the gifts it has to offer.

Paris, the City of Lights, that inspired this book

My friend Marcia and I visit the Louvre Gallery in Paris

CHAPTER ONE

50 Is Fabulous

> "To live the second half of life, alive and awake,
> from a place of wholeness and ever-expanding good."
> — Ella Croney

Why do I want to shout from the rooftops about how wonderful my life has become at age 50? Because I've watched my close friends and work associates start going through "The Change," and in most cases, including my own, it wasn't good – at least in the beginning.

One of the most traumatic experiences that ever happened to me was watching a man in the second half of his life die onboard an aircraft with two doctors, two nurses and several other medical personnel trying to revive him. This man had a heart attack and his bag was filled with heart medications. And yet he was eating a cheeseburger and chips in flight. That was to be his last meal.

I wondered why this person could have a history of heart problems and not have been given any knowledge about proper nutrition or alternative healing methods. Did he really have to die? Could he have lived longer if he had eaten healthier? Who knows? But I do know it made everyone on that flight feel the closeness of death and question what we could do to live longer, healthier lives.

Personally I had started asking these sorts of questions three years earlier when I began having horrible mood swings, broke up with my boyfriend, and didn't want anything to do with men or sex because sex itself had become numbing and sometimes painful.

My memory was lapsing and I was signing important documents incorrectly. I was misreading documents and making hasty decisions that cost me money and time. In short, I had become a total mess.

So my friends who know me wanted to know how I turned things around in less than two years. How had I ended up on an Air France flight heading for Paris in a jubilant mood to celebrate my 50th birthday?

While at the airport terminal, a young stud muffin moved three times in order to seat himself in front of me, introducing himself as Richard from Southern California. He was obviously going on my flight and asked if he could take me to dinner in Paris. It surprised me because he wasn't a day over 32. We laughed, talked, agreed to meet up in Paris and as I boarded the aircraft, the flight attendants took my coach ticket and placed me up in business class. Wow! I didn't know at the time that while I sat in the terminal, laughing and talking with other people around me and telling them I was headed for Paris for my 50th birthday, a pilot out of uniform overheard the conversation. He was working my flight and requested the flight crew move me up to business class. I was turned on like a firecracker and loving every minute of having ME back.

Six weeks before my flight to Paris, I had decided to call together a production crew, wrote a script for a Feng Shui DVD and we completed shooting it in two days. Now, I'm the same one who three years prior was losing my memory and forgetting important information. My brain was now firing like a 20-year-old in college, and I felt free.

Passion returned to me that made me fall in love with life, and amazing people showed up to make my life better than I've ever imagined. Here I was, 50 years old, had the time of my life in Paris, returned home and a gentleman friend met up with me in San Francisco, ordered a limo, and took me and my girlfriends out for a lovely dinner and night on the town.

Two weeks later, I was asked out on a date by a former NFL football player and we had so much fun that he called me the next day and said, "We're doing a spa day all day long in Beverly Hills, get ready!" Fun. Fun. Fun.

I could go on, but trust me, my life just keeps getting better and the surprises show up every day and for this, I am grateful. You couldn't pay me to want to be 20, 30, or even 40 again. Because the presence of the Goddess Venus arises and if you can ground her energy, life will take you on a magnificent adventure.

Why am I sharing my brag book? Because I want you to know we have the power and the means to turn life changes around and make them good … at any age.

Coming from a background of meditation classes, self-help books, and teacher training for spiritual growth, I prided myself on knowing techniques that could pull me out of any situation and turn my life around. I tried everything and in this newfound place of paramenopause, I was at a complete loss to find myself in an unhealthy, unhappy state off and on for almost two years.

Shocked to find myself in a state of depression, with awful symptoms of hot flashes, night sweats and mood swings accompanied by unstoppable bleeding, I was experiencing much more than I bargained for.

For the first time in my life, I couldn't find the strength to think positive thoughts or lift my own vibration to look for a brighter day, so I stayed away from people as much as I could.

I'm not sure how many weeks I stayed locked in my own negative world but, at some point, I pulled out some old meditation teaching materials to read from the Nature of the Soul Series and a peace came over me that let me know I didn't have to live that way.

So the search began.

The Wake-up Call

Twenty five years ago, when I was a stock and commodities broker, Cher, a dear friend of mine, was diagnosed with breast cancer. She went to at least five different doctors, looking for alternative treatments because she was convinced that chemo and radiation were harmful. Being raised in Hawaii around people who used herbal remedies for everything and witnessing those methods first hand, she tried to convince these doctors to help her. Sadly, she was literally thrown out of their offices and by the time she reached doctor number five, he tried to have her committed that day and did not allow her to walk out of his office. In tears, she excused herself to go to the bathroom and called me at work, crying and pleading for me to come and get her ... which I did.

When I arrived to pick her up from the doctor's office in Orange County, California, I was shocked at his rudeness and arrogance. He was yelling at both of us, but I stood in his face and said, "We are out of here. Do I look like I'm afraid of you? I don't think so."

I was fuming angry and filled with determination to help my friend to find other methods of healing her cancer and to prove that doctor wrong ... so I used my resources and connections to start researching, which was my forte as a stock broker.

To start, I came into contact with a native American Elder of the Lakota tribe who got my friend on the Essiac tea which started her detoxing program. From there, we learned about Dr. Hulda Clark and her herbs and office in Mexico, who also wrote *A Cure For All Cancers*. My friend was connected to amazing healers and physicians and research scientists through the Whole Life Expo and Mind, Body and Spirit Expo. These shows happened yearly throughout the nation. I was fascinated and happy for Cher, who was well on her way to a healthy life. She had been correct all along – there are so many alternative methods out there if you're open and receptive.

Years later, becoming ill myself from toxic poisoning and out of habit going to my conventional doctor, I ended up in the emergency room. I decided to go the non-traditional route and not be a victim of prescription drugs and their side-effects. And now, crossing the 50 year mark, I've had to return again to non-traditional methods. All of this stems from over 20 years ago, assisting Cher, and in turn helping myself and countless others. Moving from researching the markets to researching health has been a fascinating journey. Since I, too, am a part of this experience, it is my desire, my passion and privilege to share as much of this wonderful information as possible with you.

The Search Continues

Twenty years ago while I was walking down the aisle of an airplane, a gorgeous man who resembled Sydney Poitier looked up at me from an *Ebony* magazine featuring Tina Turner on the cover. He smiled and said, "This will be you in twenty years when you turn fifty."

I, of course, laughed, embarrassed at his comment and asked him what he meant. He said, "When you turn fifty, you are going to be and look fabulous in your own way, just like Tina. You're going to step into your own power and shine. I promise you this!"

Smiling, I could only say, "Well, thank you!"

Two weeks later, a world renowned psychic and palm reader was on our flight and all the flight attendants were asking for readings, except me. Finally, near the end of the flight, he looked at me and said, "You're not the least bit interested in knowing your future, are you?"

I answered, "My actions from each day will determine my future for tomorrow and when I want to change my life, all I need to do is put my attention in a new direction."

He was amazed. He then proceeded to tell me, "You may not ever marry again because there is sacred work for you to do after you raise your son, and this work will come through you and from your experiences. You will add value to other people's lives."

Okay, here I go again, I thought. As if by magic, these interesting and mysterious men showed up with wonderful messages for me to embrace. Those were my first experiences in acknowledging the gifts of the spirit.

The following day, I made sure I picked up the *Ebony* magazine with Tina Turner on the cover and a couple of other magazines featuring women who have gotten older but took great care of themselves. I found amazing pictures of Diana Ross, Sofia Loren, and other models with gray hair. Along with a photo of my own beautiful mother, I made a fabulous collage of these women and put it up in my walk-in closet, and every time I dressed, I thanked them for making growing older glamorous.

Years later, I learned much by reading a book by Deepak Chopra titled *Ageless Body-Timeless Mind,* and listening relentlessly to his tapes. Deepak spoke of research in Third World countries where people lived well past their 100-year birthdays, and they were swimming, horseback riding, dancing, loving and enjoying life so much that the young people envied them. Why? Because with their mature age and wisdom came freedom from the restraints that society places on you during your younger years. They were now in charge of their lives and living to the fullest. These amazing centenarians believed that to grow old was glamorous.

I was onto something! Having beautiful women on the collage in my closet made me feel that growing older could have its benefits, unlike the magazine articles that said if you were thirty-five and unmarried, your chances of getting hit by a Mack truck were better than attracting men. These silly notions no longer rang true for me.

I enrolled in a weekly meditation class so I could have more of an understanding of the mind, body and soul connection. Surely the true stories in Deepak's books and tapes had much more to them than meets the eye. This all became so fascinating to me that I also studied with other teachers – courses such as Corrective Thinking, The Soul and Its Instrument, Nature of The Soul and from there went on to two more years of teacher's training. Studying these meditation series opened my mind to how we live, move, and attend to our beingness.

My studies helped me realize that something or someone is always going to impact us or influence our way of thinking. When we are young, we are very impressionable. The question is, will we be impacted in a positive or negative way? I didn't think we would still be easily impressed this way as adults, but that's what advertisers do to us all the time! The handsome man on the airplane that day who looked like Sydney Poitier and showed me the picture of Tina Turner impacted my life with an idea completely different from what we've been taught in the U.S. The passion behind his words let me know that I could grow older, look good, and most of all, feel great!

And now, here I am at fifty years of age having more fun than I ever imagined possible, being pursued by more men than is allowed by law, being more creative than I ever was before, taking motivational courses, breaking wood with my bare hands, walking across coals of fire. And there's more ... I returned to school and studied TV and film production, producing a cable TV show featuring my son's first CD about positive hip hop, and titled the show *Hip Hop with a Healthy Spirit*. I took a three month Feng Shui course with a Master and started my own Feng Shui consultation business. I have so many successful stories from my clients that I will be writing them in a book.

What I know for sure is there are still so many unlimited possibilities available for us even in the second half of our lives and maybe more so than our earlier years. At this stage and this age, we don't have to prove anything to anyone but ourselves. On this path, baby, you can have your cake and eat it too!

The Past Meets the Present

At age thirteen, still wearing a training bra, I found lumps under my arms and in my breast.

"Mom! Mom!" I cried out from the bathroom and she came running in to see the look of panic on my face. My wonderful Mom tried to calm me down as I lifted my arms so she could check for me and sure enough, she felt the lumps also. There were a total of three lumps - two on my right breast, one on my left.

The next day at the hospital, she waited patiently as the doctor examined me and asked her to step outside with him. My Mom returned with the news that we had to schedule an operation the very next week. This is not something a parent or child wants to hear, but we handled it, feeling assured that all would go well.

As it turned out, the breast cysts were benign. All that was left after the operation were two little pencil scars, yet the doctor let me know, "In the future when you decide to have children, those little scars will stretch and become much larger."

At thirteen years of age and not having had sex, the thought of ever having children wasn't even part of my program. I was still a bit of a tomboy, climbing trees, going fishing with my male cousins and building tree houses. Some good things do come to an end.

I forgot about the incident, got on with my life and graduated high school early at age 16 because I was bored and wanted to get out of school. Period! During my graduation, my boyfriend, a grade school sweetheart, returned home from military leave and asked my mother for my hand in marriage and, of course, proposed to me. "Yes!" I said. Not only was I getting out of school, I was leaving Kentucky on the first airplane to Cadiz, Spain. I tell you, I thought to myself, *Girl, you must be living right!*

Our honeymoon in Spain lasted about two years and I even gave birth to our wonderful son there. And just as the doctor had announced a few years earlier, those little pencil marks stretched and became large during my pregnancy and a bit uncomfortable.

I thought briefly, *What else is in store with these scars?* And by the time I was 23 years of age, exactly ten years later, more lumps returned and this time, instead of only three lumps under those scars, there were seven!

At this point, I was living in California with a small child, having recently divorced. The doctors explained only that I was one in a million women who over-produced something in their bodies that created these cysts. Again I had them surgically removed, this time as an outpatient.

By now, my life had become much more hectic, my being a single mom alone in California, without family, trying to raise my son on my own, working full-time and trying to stay sane. Around this time, a friend introduced me to the practice of meditation. This wasn't something spoken of in the hardcore Baptist Church of my upbringing, but, as I looked at the lives of others from that same indoctrination, their lives weren't looking too good either.

The meditation course I was taking helped me hold a focus and reclaim my mind, which I certainly wasn't able to do by myself. The course met weekly and I so looked forward to the timeout for myself. I began to notice during these calming times just how much drama had played a major role in my life experiences. Havoc from my childhood was still causing mishaps in my adult life. I wondered how this could be. Finally, I was able to pull back and look at my own life from a different perspective, which in turn led me to believe I could make new choices today that would affect my life in years to come. This felt profound to me.

Nine or ten years later, having been practicing meditation and learning more about eating healthier for energy, again I had no idea of the depth that healthy eating choices would take me. I wanted to try something to keep me going through the tough years of juggling motherhood, working, being involved in my son's school, teaching Sunday school and just trying to keep my head above water.

Just when I thought things were moving along at a pace I could handle, Bam! Those lumps showed up again in the same exact areas but this time, we're talking about sixteen new ones. I went into full panic mode, totally angry for having to deal with this problem for a third time, and for some reason, I was determined this time to research and find more answers. That week, at another group meditation course for teachers, I asked if anyone knew anything about breast cysts, and was there another way to deal with this other than surgically, since I had already been through this twice.

It turns out that my teacher herself had used alternative methods to put her cancer in remission. She sent me to her chiropractor who used a different method call Applied Kinesiology. There were actually two different doctors using this method – Dr. Karen Bolin in Tustin and Dr. Robert Eberle in Laguna Hills, both in California, of course. I had been to a chiropractor before and didn't understand why my instructor had suggested them to me, but she assured me their approach was much different.

I started out with Dr. Karen, who did some treatments on me and, yes, they were very different than anything else I'd encountered. She put me on a six-week diet of no sugar, no bread, no caffeine. I had to use extra vitamin E (400 instead of my usual 200 units) along with evening primrose oil, flax oil, and lots of fish. Salmon was at the top of my list, which happened to be my favorite. Giving up the coffee was absolute hell, along with my usual morning donuts or croissants on my way to work.

Eating more salads was easy, along with more vegetables with my salmon or sometimes chicken. I had to replace my morning cup of Joe with herbal teas and that was not easy but I was willing to try anything to understand my body and why I had these recurring cysts that came back every nine or ten years.

I made it through three weeks on my diet program, but by the end of week three, I called Dr. Karen and said, "If you don't let me have a croissant with at least a cup of decaf coffee, I'm coming into the office to pull your hair out!"

She laughed and said, "Go ahead and treat yourself this time and continue on your diet afterwards."

Lo and behold, I had my decaf coffee with Stevia, a natural, healthier sweetener I'd learned about. The funny thing was, the croissant was buttery and I ate it slowly as she suggested, and didn't even eat it all. I knew then I could continue my program.

Interestingly, by week five, my sugar cravings no longer existed and there were only three small lumps total out of the sixteen, and by week six of my diet, I had energy like you can't believe. I returned to Dr. Karen for another treatment and, voila! there were no more lumps to be found. Amazing! This was my first true experience with the mind-body connection because, along with the doctors' treatments, my meditation teacher was guiding me through visualization techniques, showing me how to bring in light and love throughout my body, with heavy concentration on my breast area and how to bring calmness to my emotions.

I honestly had no clue that all the junk food I had been eating was creating this mishap in my body. Sadly to say, I could have gone back to one of my old doctors and again had those lumps surgically removed without changing any of my old habits of bad eating. And within ten years or so, who knows how much worse this situation could have become. Not one conventional doctor had ever spoken to me about my diet, the sugary foods I was constantly eating, or the emotional ups and downs I was going through as a single parent.

I had no idea that growing up surrounded by family drama – both parents alcoholics – and a mother who was consistently abused physically and emotionally, and myself being the oldest child taking over her responsibilities when she was drunk. If that wasn't enough, I spent my young life being afraid to come home from school on Fridays because Friday was when the drinking started and I wouldn't know what I would walk into at home – like a mother with a broken jaw or a broken arm or busted ribs, or possibly dead. What a horrible way to live as a child, yet I did this for years.

So here it was, twenty years later, that I found myself as a volunteer at a workshop given by the Learning Light Foundation in Anaheim, California, with Joe Dispenza from the movie *What the Bleep* as the guest speaker. As I listened to his presentation, he said something that rocked my world. "Your parents are great drama teachers and if you want to know what your life will be like when you get older, take a look at your parents – their beliefs and habits, good ones and bad ones."

In a nutshell (and I am paraphrasing here) if you want to grow old, fall apart at the seams, be on prescription drugs for the rest of your life, have a host of surgeries, then continue doing what you've been taught – do nothing. And you'll be a carbon copy of your parents.

On the other hand, if you choose to use your brain and seek out new options for your health and well-being, you can make the necessary changes now that can ensure a longer, healthier life for your future that will be much more productive and balanced than your parents ever dreamed of.

This proved to be only the beginning of learning about and using alternative healing methods which I will joyfully share with you throughout this book, in hopes you will ask new questions and gain more insight about your amazing body before having something cut out of you as I did … twice. This information will not only help you live longer, but healthier and happier along the way.

The body-mind-soul connection requires Intention, Attention, and Observation.

> "We move from thinking to doing to being."
> — Joe Dispenza D.C., from Evolve Your Brain

"Whoever told us that joy was for the young,
Or fun is for the young,
Or freedom is for the young,
Or adventure is for the young?
The truth be told, all of this and more
Is for the young at heart.
Age is only a number,
And its meaning is what you give it
Nothing more, nothing less."
—Ella Croney

CHAPTER TWO

Applied Kinesiology

Women of age, there is hope out there for going through 'the Change' and getting help with menopause! My own experience involved missing periods, then having periods that lasted 20 to 24 days straight. That sent me to my traditional doctor, an M.D., to have blood tests done that showed no signs of the changes my body was going through! Well, it was obvious his tests and my body were saying two different things, and he, of course, was convinced from his tests that I was not going through the Change.

One night I ended up in the Emergency Room, weak and anemic from so many days of excess blood flow. The ER doctor, a female, said, "Yes, you are para-menopausal and there's a well-known clinic nearby you could visit tomorrow. They work with women going through the Change."

The very next morning, I was in that clinic with a new doctor who told me the best way to handle my situation was to have a scraping of the wall of the uterus. (Pain, pain, ladies, true pain!) I tried it in spite of my misgivings because I was willing to do anything to stop the bleeding. The doctor at the clinic also placed me on birth control pills to normalize my periods again and voila! his method worked. I was so grateful ... and for the next three weeks, I was sure I had my life back.

One afternoon, while I was having a fun lunch with a friend, I felt a warm, heavy feeling and ran to the restroom to discover I had started my period without any warning whatsoever. I thought, *Please, not again!* and sure enough by Day 10, the vicious cycle of previous months had started to repeat itself.

After another agonizing night of worry and bodily discomfort, I called my favorite chiropractor, Dr. Eberle. He had worked with me in the past through a food poisoning incident and an episode of toxic air inhalation, detoxing and rebalancing my body. We had a good history of working together. I felt like the traditional methods hadn't worked for me and I was hoping that this time, there was something Dr. Eberle could do, even though this was a new and different dilemma.

Dr. Eberle was in his office at 7 o'clock the next morning when I called. He told me, "Come on in, you don't sound good."

Now, Dr. Eberle's approach uses a method known as Applied Kinesiology (see more detail at end of chapter), which involves working with the different bodily systems. He began working on me and saw that all my muscle groups and internal organs of the stomach were showing weak. He immediately took me off the birth control pills, and had me take home a saliva test kit to use at all my meals. When the test was sent in, the results showed that I was over-producing progesterone, and I also had way too much soy in my system. I had to stop using everything with soy in it – my protein powder, my soy milk, soy butter, soy yogurt, you name it!

Dr. Eberle placed me on an amazing herb called Adaptocrine (K-2) for adrenal support to stop the excessive bleeding, help alleviate the vaginal dryness, and stop the hot flashes. Dr. Eberle thought it would take two or three months for the Adaptocrine to take effect, but it began working within two weeks. I used it along with Susun Weed's tea infusions. The night sweats stopped, the mood swings were history and the hot flashes were a thing of the past.

Over the years, I have sent several other women to see Dr. Eberle for various reasons. He was the doctor who one of my meditation teachers used, along with Dr. Karen Bolin, to help put her breast cancer into remission. Another wonderful friend who had radiation treatments in a Newport Beach hospital would leave the hospital to go to Dr. Eberle's office, receive treatments from him, use the herbs he gave her to balance, leave his office and go to the gym to work out. Her doctors at the hospital were amazed that her blood count always read normal, and she never got weak like their other patients. When she tried to tell them about Dr. Eberle's treatments, they just turned and walked away.

Ladies, there are so many more alternatives out there for us to choose from, and if you find yourself tired of the old traditional methods that aren't working, you now have options.

Another great benefit from using the Adaptocrine is that it helps to get rid of that middle stomach bulge that shows up during the Change. Yeah! My friend from Canada called after using this product for a few weeks and said, "I have my curves back!" In fact, she sang it into my phone and I laughed out loud.

If there are any skeptics out there, I can vouch, from 20 years of experiencing these treatments on and off whenever necessary for a wide variety of reasons, that this work is truly heaven sent for my friends, clients and family members. I am grateful at age 50 to have my beautiful body back that looks good and feels marvelous. Voila!

From Dr. Eberle's Office for those who need to know a little more about Applied Kinesiology:

"During the 1960s, a new system of evaluation began to develop in chiropractic. Dr. George Goodheart of Detroit, MI, found that evaluation of normal and abnormal body function could be accomplished by using muscle tests. Since the original discovery, this system has expanded to include the nervous, vascular, and lymphatic systems, nutrition, acupuncture, cerebrospinal fluids function and many other controlling or disturbing factors that influence health. This system is called Applied Kinesiology."

Further evaluation by the doctor reveals the 'controlling' factor, the 'weakness' in what area of the body might be at fault, and what treatment is necessary to return to normal function.

For more information, read online about Applied Kinesiology. Contacts:

Los Angeles County, CA	Orange County, CA
Dr. Adam Thropay	Dr. Robert Eberle
11425 Paramount Blvd.	23276 South Pt. 110
Downey, CA 90241	Laguna Hills, CA
562/861-3896	949/770-5052

NAET

Allergies are something I never paid much attention to until my second year of working as a flight attendant. I began to notice that within an hour or so of being on the airplane, I would start to have sniffles, be sneezing, with a runny nose and before the flight ended, my eyes would be itching. I couldn't put my finger on what exactly was causing these discomforts, so I began recording all my symptoms, along with noticing that, at least twice per year, I'd get hit with a bad cold or flu, even though I had taken the flu shots. In speaking with other senior flight attendants, I learned that this was something they all experienced to acclimate to their environment. This wasn't good news.

My allergies got so bad that anything I ate from the airplane would cause havoc – a skin rash or a yeast or bladder infection. And I started having tooth and gum problems.

My treatment for these symptoms started with my conventional doctor who gave me antibiotics off and on, which just made my yeast infections worsen. Finally, the doctor said, "It must be your boyfriend giving this back to you." The problem was, I hadn't had a boyfriend or lover in the year or so before and during these problems, so obviously it was time for me to try another route.

I started asking healers if they knew of any other methods. That is how I discovered NAET.

It turned out that several flight attendants often used this method but weren't willing to openly speak about it because it was not conventional medicine. One lady I met personally had developed such bad yeast problems that she had to take off work and keep her hands covered for months at a time, even during her wedding!

Her husband, an EMT, had heard about Dr. Devi Nambutripad through outside sources and was willing to help his wife try anything within reason because the conventional methods hadn't helped her at all. They were very informative and assured me it would be different than anything I'd ever done, but to go ahead and try it as it worked for them. His loving wife was living yeast free and back to work, and, of course, not having to wear gloves every time she went out. Mind you, this young lady was in her early 30s with those symptoms.

Within a week, I was in Dr. Devi's office. She is an amazing woman who is an M.D., D.C., L.Ac, Ph.D.(Acu.), and the inventor of NAET, or Nambudripad's Allergy Elimination Techniques. I had my first series of treatments with Dr. Devi and her husband, Chris, and her sister, Mala.

Upon my initial testing, we discovered that my body wasn't even assimilating the vitamins I was taking, which explained part of the fatigue I constantly felt. We used an instrument that manipulated the spine for our treatments, along with specific acupuncture points being treated at the same time.

The beginning sessions started out with a group of vitamins in a vial to help rebuild my immune system. Later we went on to specifics, such as sugar, yeast and preservatives from the foods I ate on the airplane.

Within four weeks, after a visit or twice weekly, my fatigue lifted and the yeast infections cleared up. I became much more in tune with how my body was affected by processed foods. Three months later, I was able to go in from time to time as needed when I felt a bit out of sorts, and it would always be related to something I'd eaten on an airplane. Needless to say, I started, as much as I could, to take home-cooked food to work. I also learned how to use muscle testing to read my body's allergy response to eating out when I was in restaurants.

Many of my friends and their children have been helped using this method for various reasons, including milk, peanut, yeast, sugar, alcohol, wheat, preservatives and even water allergies that have been cleared for years at a time and, in some cases, have been eliminated completely.

If you or someone you know has suffered off and on for years with allergies, NAET is definitely worth looking into. It's safe for children and adults and, instead of masking the problem as in conventional methods, NAET finds what's underneath the problem and works with the body to clear that symptom.

> "We know that most illnesses (i.e., headaches, joint pains, addictions, PMS, indigestion, body aches, etc.) are caused by undiagnosed allergies. When left untreated, allergies can become serious, life-threatening illnesses."
>
> — Dr. Devi

Mala has been doing amazing work for parents with children who are having ADD problems without medicating them as conventional doctors are doing. In this day and age, when so many parents have children being put on prescription drugs that turn them into adults who can't cope with life, this method is worth its weight in gold.

If you have any fear of these new flu situations that have entered our country – the Birdie Flu or the Piggy Flu – I would use NAET first before allowing myself or my loved ones to get shots that may cause serious issues down the line or may not even work.

My dear friend Rosemary is a living, walking testimonial that NAET has worked for her when the conventional doctors gave up on her. She has amazing stories to share about how NAET helped to bring her out of a major illness to live a joyous full life. Rosemary is truly the life of any party and she loves sharing this method with anyone who will listen because we both know, as do hundreds of others, that it works.

Dr. Devi's book *Say Goodbye to Illness* explains more about this revolutionary treatment. Dr. Devi's son and his wife, are running the office and doing a great service for all whom are blessed to have this amazing technique available. Say Ella Croney sent you! [www.NAET.com 714/523-0800]

In my new book, "HEALTHY TIPS ON THE RUN," I shared some newfound information about "Total Body Modification." This system combines the above methods and does so much more.

My friends, family and clients have had successful results with TBM.

My contact - Dr.Robert Nolan 1(714)633-5521 www.nolanchiro.com

www.amazon.com/dp/B013HIHZHW. visit www.TBM.com for a doctor near you.

"Masking problems with medications have led this country to fall short when it comes to health and healing. Our bodies and our minds are now paying a very high price.

"We now have the methods and support to take back our power and live healthy lives. Saying goodbye to illness is now within our reach."

— Ella Croney

Tea Infusions:

Menopause – a gift to a new, empowered you.

When someone asks, "Where's my juice? I ask, "Where's my energy? And why does it feel like it's in my shoes?"

I had found a way to balance my menstrual flow working with Dr. Eberle using Applied Kinesiology, and yet my hair took on a dullness I didn't like, and my skin was always dry, along with vaginal dryness (not fun), and sometimes aching bones.

What was this para-menopause crap? And why was it messing with my mojo?

I started thinking about all the herbal formulas on the market and knew there had to be some that addressed women's issues similar to what I was going through. One day, as I entered the door of my health food store, an *Awareness* magazine on the rack caught my eye. A Native American woman on the cover – Susun Weed – was being interviewed about women going through the Change, and what natural remedies there were to help. This article was a gift beyond my wildest dreams.

It was written by Randy Peyser, introducing Susun Weed as an herbalist from upstate New York, who teaches a traditional course – The Wise Women's Way. In the article, of course, she shared women's concerns with menopause and how they can stay healthy while going through the process and afterwards. She spoke about the health of our bones and breasts and how to stay juicy. She introduced me to her herbal formulas, called Tea Infusions, made from herbs such as nettle, red clover, and oat straw.

That very day, I purchased the dry herbs from my health food store and took them home to mix and use. These are not your 'pour over a cup of water' tea bags.

I started with the stinging nettle and immediately noticed a shift in my mood and energy. The stinging nettle added more support for my adrenals, along with more minerals and protein in my diet.

In the second week of using these teas, I tried the red clover, which turned out to be another good energy booster, good for your heart and breasts. It was easier to get myself out and exercise again. And interestingly, I had stopped craving sweets.

The third week, I changed over to the oat straw, which is supposed to be good for making us juicy again in the right places. Wow, yes it worked, along with making my hair shine and my skin baby-smooth again. Whatever was happening with my aching bones completely stopped by my third week of using these tea infusions.

I am forever grateful to Randy Peyser for writing and sharing this article in *Awareness* magazine. (www.awarenessmag.com) Randy also edits books and helps authors find agents and publishers. Her site is: www.randypeyser.com.

For the recipe for mixing the tea infusions, contact Susun Weed at: www.herbshealing.com, www.susunweed.com And say hello for me!

There are many natural ways such as these for women and men that help us go through our changes, strong and beautiful.

CHAPTER THREE

Get More Oxygen

Why oxygen? Because diseases, yeast infections, cancers, HIV and various other illnesses can only live in an oxygen-deprived body. People often return from their air travels not quite feeling well, with a slight cold, sniffles or just plain fatigued … and they haven't accounted for the fact that the amount of oxygen they were breathing during and after their trip had been cut dramatically, and it made them more susceptible to picking up various bugs.

I am speaking as a veteran flight-attendant with a job in an enclosed environment where the air is recirculated and germs are thriving. It doesn't matter if you're traveling for vacation or business, the moment you get on an aircraft with the doors closed, you're vulnerable.

I honestly didn't know about vitamin C drips, hyperbaric chambers, ozone therapies and chelation therapy until I became a flight attendant and met frequent business travelers who shared how they stayed healthy using these alternative methods. Sadly, they are much more readily available in other countries where preventive medicine is more common. The benefits of using any of these methods are amazing and the prices are reasonable, which is the reason they are not readily advertised in our country.

It is important that you check with qualified, professional holistic doctors, naturopaths, preventive medical clinics and healer referrals before you venture into this unknown territory.

We are constantly bombarded with more toxic chemicals and pollution in our everyday lives than ever before in the history of our country, and it's proven by the high number of cancers, obesity, chronic fatigue and other discomforts that are now part of the fabric of our lives.

A good friend was being treated at UCLA medical center for breast cancer when her doctor told her, "If you were living in a Third World country, you would not be in my office with breast cancer." Wow! Now that's something to contemplate. He talked about how the soil in Third World countries is still rich in nutrients and the spraying of chemicals does not occur. And the injection of hormones into meat is unheard of and they don't need food coloring on vegetables to make them look good. And we in this country think we're so above others!

My friend was amazed at what she was hearing from this renowned doctor from UCLA. He went on to share with her the damaging effects of diet colas on the brain over a long period of time. She walked away from her appointment in a daze, yet filled with hope because he made her more aware of the body/mind connection, and of the benefits of eating healthier and living a more balanced life.

Her experience made me wonder about visiting other countries, and eating salads that taste really good, having desserts that are not nearly as sweet and never as large as the portions of food we consume here in the U.S., thinking there's something wrong if there's not a large portion of food on our plates, even if it has very little health value for our bodies. In turn, the body gets too acidic and starves for oxygen, which opens a doorway for diseases of all sorts to enter our bodily environment.

I will gladly share some of my findings and experiences for adding more oxygen to our lives because nothing deadly can live in an oxygen-rich body. There is a fabulous book out entitled *Flood Your Body with Oxygen*, by Ed McCabe. Please read it.

There are oxygenated waters at health food stores, along with oxygen pills and drops you can add to your water (one brand is called ChlorOxygen), which has chlorophyll concentrate, which gives your body oxygen. There are also dark, rich green vegetables that feed oxygen to your cells.

"When you feed your body with oxygen, you are choosing Life."
— Ed McCabe, Flood Your Body with Oxygen

Next, let's look at more therapeutic ways to receive oxygen, as in hyperbaric oxygen and ozone therapies, chelation therapy and lymphatic cleanses, how they work and if they can work for you for preventive medicine and /or to add to your treatments for any illness that may be present in your life at this time.

> TO THY OWN SELF BE TRUE.
> DOCTOR, HEAL THYSELF

Ozone Therapy

Ozone oxygen treatments really revitalized my life. I used to fly to Arizona just for the day to have spa treatments done because California doesn't allow IV-ozone treatments.

The cost of these ozone treatments for preventive medicine along with attacking major illnesses within the body temple (including depression, fatigue, strokes, lupus, cancers and AIDS) is less than $200 per treatment (not covered by insurance, however). Compare that cost to the costs of radiation and chemotherapy and, of course, the cost of the pharmaceutical drugs that are also a part of that process.

Ozone has been used for many years by German doctors who claim its benefits in scientific and clinical studies. In some clinics around the world, ozone is the first agent administered to each patient entering the clinic, no matter what their illness is.

Ozone is a medical therapy introduced into our bodies. It is O3 and we normally breathe O2.

As I mentioned previously being a flight attendant for 20 years and having been exposed to a bad air quality incident was enough to let me know I didn't want to take any risks with my health, so this was a wonderful way to add more oxygen to my body temple directly through the blood as a safety factor, and for preventive long-term health.

There are several ways to get more oxygen into the cells, but I prefer this: having a nurse at the clinic remove a small portion of my blood in an IV tube, ozone it, and slowly IV-drip it back into my body. I have also tried ozone saunas, but the results from the saunas weren't even noticeable. The results from the IV ozone-drip were amazing and stayed with me for weeks at a time. My energy level soars after the IV-ozone treatments, my mental clarity comes back, my eyesight improves, and I exercise with a feeling of 'being in the flow.' I breathe deeply and fully again. It is a tremendous boost for my immune system because it's detoxifying the body and cleaning the blood.

People who love to travel in airplanes are now aware of long flights and the possibility of forming blood clots. My naturopathic doctor found blood clots from my testing. The ozone has proven to be a perfect way to increase the blood circulation throughout my body. After one treatment, there were no more signs of blood clots.

Ozone using the IV method is only allowed in certain states, so go online and research the area where you live. I only receive the ozone treatments every 3 or 4 months for preventive measures, and it has made a tremendous difference in my life and for my flying career by eliminating fatigue.

This is for information only, and not medical advice. Be intelligent and consult with a health practitioner or naturopathic doctor before trying this or other alternative methods.

Dr. Zermeno often reminds us that it's not only what we put in our bodies, but also what we take out. This is important because Ozone stimulates detoxication and increases oxygenation, allowing the body to repair damaged areas.

My contact in Southern California for Ozone and Integrative Medicine is Dr. German Zermeno, M.D. (657) 231-6164

"It's good to feel good and to know you have more options to live a quality life.
To not have the knowledge and be aware of these methods is one thing, to not take advantage of them is another."

-Ella Croney

Lymphatic Cleanse

Toxins are everywhere – in the water you brush your teeth with, the water you shower with. You breathe in toxins every day just being inside your home, cleaning your home. Using everyday toxic products from under your kitchen sink produces so many toxins, it's enough to make you and your children ill. Putting gas in your car and just being around smokers are also sources of toxicity in the air you breathe.

Once a year, I treat myself to an internal spa day at Cove Wellness in La Jolla, CA. It's not a foo-foo place, but truly where you go to rid your lymphatic system of toxins, along with cleaning out your colon. Sessions end with a therapeutic foot soak, where the water starts out clear and ends up sometimes brown, sometimes red, or green according to what toxins you've built up in your body system.

A female friend had breast cancer, with swollen lymph nodes, went to the center. Before she'd finished, her swollen arm had gone down and the clear water had turned red in clearing up her blood clotting.

> "Detox, detox and detox again. The lymphatic system is often considered our circulatory system. It consists of a network of vessels carrying the lymph (water, proteins and electrolytes) from the tissue fluids to the bloodstream. It supports us in keeping our bloodstream healthy, which makes the lymphatic system important in the elimination of toxins.
> Many factors lead to lymph blockage, such as stress, hormonal imbalance, chemical toxicity and unhealthy diets."
> — Cove Wellness

I've known for years that the fun environment of the airline business I've chosen to work in is also a toxic environment. I was willing to try anything I could do to keep my system cleansed and stay as healthy as possible under the circumstances.

If you know how good you feel after a massage, then this technology known as vibrational science for the lymphatic cleanse will leave you glowing and floating on air for days and days.

At Cove Wellness, some of the commonly treated symptoms are fibromyalgia, parasites, Candida, breast congestion, chronic constipation, prostate health and rheumatoid arthritis.

For me and many of my friends, this is just another preventive method to help ourselves stay strong and healthy in the second half of our lives.

Contact: Lisa at:
Cove Wellness Inner Beauty Center of La Jolla
7946 Ivanhoe Ave. Ste. #202 (El Patio Building)
1-858-551-9228, https://www.covewellness.com/

Say hello to Lisa and the staff and tell them Ella the flight attendant sent you!

"Wherever the art of medicine is loved, there is also love of humanity."

-Hippocrates

CHAPTER FOUR

Deep Internal Cleansing

If you're 38 and people think you look 45, or if you're 42 and people think you look 55, this could point to a need for a lifestyle change.

When you can't drag yourself off the sofa all weekend and you're eating potato chips, cookies and ice-cream, eating junk foods and drinking colas, you're probably depressed and won't bother exercising. Welcome to the club with the all-American bad diet habit of comfort food. You could have a colon problem brewing.

You can waste your time blaming your bad diet habits on your bad job, or no job, or your bad marriage, or whatever you wish, but it all comes back to taking responsibility for your health and your life.

Here's the big one: if you have no sex drive or no sexual desire that, too, could be a clue that your colon is overloaded with backed-up garbage and your blood stream is filled with toxins, and, of course, your liver is dirty. Wake up, America! This is not the time to pop another sleeping pill, or pull the covers over your head and hope your ailments will disappear. It's time to clean your body from the inside out. Colon cleansing, also referred to as colonic irrigations, is the path to take.

A colonic is done by a professional using state-of-the-art equipment to reach areas that regular enemas can't. It involves a gentle pumping of warm water into the bowels. You can go online and read more about this method to determine if it can work for you.

Marcia and I have fun in Paris with our French waiter

"Colon cleansing allows for a cleaner bloodstream, improved digestion and elimination, greater vitality and better assimilation of vital nutrients."

— Cove Wellness of La Jolla, CA

I was in such a toxic overload that I had three colonics within one month. The worms, the mucus, the old fecal matter that came out of me was frightening. After the sessions, the feeling of having my energy back was well worth doing this for me. I also learned how we store old memories in our bodies and that this slows us down mentally and physically, and drains us emotionally. Our brains want to be free to assist us in creating new possibilities for our lives, but we can't think through the fog. I had all these symptoms and more. After my third colonic, my eyesight improved and my sugar cravings dropped dramatically, along with my blood sugar rebalancing itself. It's amazing how the body wants to help us heal itself.

Bad gas, bloating, bad breath and constipation are no fun but very common symptoms among flight attendants and pilots, or anyone frequently on an airplane. It could be the trapped air in the cabin itself along with many other variables. There's also a problem with absorption of nutrients. After being tested by my allergist (see NAET - Chapter Two), we discovered that all of the vitamins and herbs I was using weren't even being digested. My hair had become very dull with split ends, and my nails broke and chipped constantly. Something had to be done.

So along with using the NAET, I started having colonics. I was told by a naturopathic doctor at a health convention that all healing programs should start with good colon cleansing. Colonics was at the top of his list, so I contacted an amazing nurse who worked with me. I didn't know that the colon was the last portion of the digestive system and it helps you absorb your water and nutrients from good food, vitamins and herbs.

I was always sluggish after a meal, with breath problems, recurring yeast infections, liver and lower back pain. I couldn't believe how these things started clearing up on their own, along with no longer feeling depressed. I had to learn about this and other cleansing methods because of all the preservatives in the airplane food I was eating at least three days a week. You and I know that putting additives and preservatives in our foods is a common practice here in the U.S. We've already discussed how the overuse of sugar in our foods is staggering and that it works against us for keeping our colon healthy with friendly bacteria.

Google 'colonic irrigation' to bring up almost a million Internet sites, or go to:

www.colonhealth.net and choose 'Therapist search' to find an office near you.

A few contacts in Southern California:

www.covewellness.com – La Jolla, CA

Holistic Balance Studio,1-714-544-6554/cell-1-714-397-1019

www.BodyZalive.com – Santa Monica, CA

Lucky for all of us, Beate's Holistic Balance Studio offers her clients many other services along with, Colonhydro-therapy; coffee enema's; probiotic implants (Certification:(www.i-act.org); Bemer Vascular therapy; Ionic foot therapy and much more.

Coffee Enemas

When you wake up angry or irritated for no reason at all and your excuse is that you just got out on the wrong side of the bed, don't believe it! You could have eaten something the night before that didn't digest properly and your liver is overtaxed and dirty, which the Chinese say will put you in a bad mood. Coffee enemas are great because you can do them in the privacy of your home. Organic coffee cleanses and detoxifies your liver when used in an enema bucket.

The liver itself is a major blood reservoir, filtering toxins for you every minute. It will take about six enemas to equal one colonic, so why not just use your one coffee enema for liver cleansing and have a professional do you're colonic for you.

We overwork the liver by eating sugary foods, and drinking too much alcohol. The liver goes into overload, the lower back hurts or your right side aches or your arm or some body part becomes inflamed. These problems show up in the body/mind system as anger or irritability.

Doing a coffee enema at least once a week, along with using milk thistle and herbs you can get at any health food store, will lift your mood ... and possibly everyone else around you will be happier and more helpful.

Taking care of your liver is as important as a colon cleanse. They both support each other's functions. The question is not how long you want to live, but how good you want the life you're living to be. Start small, where you are loving your liver and loving your life.

Purchase an enema bucket at any drug-store. Brew a pot of organic coffee with filtered water, let it cool down or add cool water, then lie in a bathtub on your right side, insert small tube from the enema package, into your buttocks, slowly let it flow in. Try to hold the coffee inside for ten to fifteen minutes, then get on the toilet and release. This method cleanses the liver and colon. For other ways to do coffee enemas, do a Google search at www.coffee-enemas.com

Cleansing Formulas

So much information is available about good, healthy ways to rid toxins from your liver and colon. Start with a visit to a good neighborhood health food store. Read the reference books available there and talk with their personnel about different brands that fit what you are seeking at the time. Of course, your best alternative would be to start with a naturopath or holistic doctor to find out more specifically what your body needs to reach its peak performance and maintain that level of health.

One of my favorite formulas for internal cleanses is a product called Ultimate Cleanse by Nature's Secret. It consists of an AM/ PM set of herbs to start you off slowly using one in the morning and one at night to build yourself up:

Part 1 - Cleansing blend with herbs that support the body's detoxifying process.

Part 2 - Cleansing blend with fiber supports digestion and elimination. For those seeking weight loss, this product is heaven sent and your energy levels will soar, but you must train yourself to drink the full eight glasses of water for the product to work properly.

These products by Nature's Secret are not to be taken for long periods of time. A good thing to start along with these products is Arbonne's Hybrids for women or men. We'll touch on that information later and the great health benefits they have for people over 40 years of age.

Another cleansing formula I like is by Dr. Schulze. His Intestinal #1 and #2 will rock your world! Go online and read about his products; and ask for a free "Get Well" CD from his company at 1-800-HERB-DOC (437-2362).

Dr. Schulze's Intestinal Formula #1 helps eliminate constipation and promotes regular, healthy and complete bowel movements, stimulating and strengthening the muscular movement of the colon.

Dr. Schulze's Intestinal Formula #2 is a powerful intestinal vacuum that draws out old fecal matter, toxins, poisons, bacteria, drug residues, mercury and lead, and is a strong anti-inflammatory and soothing agent.

Visit his website, www.herbdoc.com, and ask for a free Catalog and CD also. Say hello from Ella.

Dr. Schulze's Liver-Gall Bladder, Female and Male Products

Dr. Schulze's Intestinal Formula #1, #2 and #3 Products

CHAPTER FIVE

Herbs

The importance of vitamins should be at the top of everyone's list; you should have herbs, oils and vitamins as a natural part of your daily routine. Why? Because our country's soil is at least 25% depleted of its vitamin content.

Women need vitamins and herbs to support breast health and menopause symptoms, and men need them to treat high blood pressure and high cholesterol. And to ensure prostate health, extra immune support is absolutely a necessity.

Remember, everything is a habit, good or bad, and slowing down long enough to take care of you is a habit that is good. Yet few men and women do slow down unless forced to do so. Don't wait. Be a better role model for your daughters and sons.

When the four cysts in my breast returned after having them surgically removed ten years earlier, twice, I was told to increase Vitamin E oil and EPA oils, along with evening primrose oil. The same thing occurred to a realtor friend from Florida.

There's something to the fact that my chiropractor here in California put me on the same oils as my friend's holistic doctor had her using in Florida. We were both able to get rid of the breast cysts and they have never returned! This is essential basic information for all women to know and use.

For men, EPA oils and pomegranate juice are great for supporting prostate health. Organic oatmeal helps lower cholesterol. Add a little raw honey to help relieve some arthritis symptoms.

I must admit I was uncomfortable when my doctor had me open ten capsules (equivalent to a teaspoon) of evening primrose oil and use them daily along with two 400 IU of the vitamin E. She monitored me closely and it worked like magic.

Some of the other benefits were that my skin became baby-soft again, and I was constantly receiving compliments from both men and women who asked me if I got facials and who was doing them for me. The skin all over my body just became silky smooth and my breasts became full and soft, minus the lumps. During that period, my menstrual cramps also became non-existent.

Please, do your research. Look into these oils at your local health food stores and speak with your healers and holistic doctors. These inexpensive oils have value beyond belief.

Herbs from the Kitchen

Herbs, spices and essential oils have been used for thousands of years, and play a permanent role in our everyday lives. For more information, check out www.youngliving.com.

From Mother's Market and Kitchen – Nutrition News:

Basil can be used to refresh the mind and restore mental alertness. It was originally used as a tea for its seductive effect and relieving headaches. Basil helps digestion and alleviates stomach cramps, and constipation. As an essential oil, Basil restricts the growth of numerous bacteria.

Parsley is the world's most popular herb, it has been given credit for supporting the kidneys and liver. We eat it after meals to sweeten the breath. The Germans use parsley root as a tea for treatment of kidney stones.

Sage is used for canker sores, carpal tunnel syndrome, gingivitis and as a douche for yeast infections. Clary sage essential oil helps with both PMS and menopause.

Thyme contains more than a dozen antiseptic compounds and is good for treating infections of the chest and respiratory system.

Grounding is an excellent essential oil blend for flight personal, as it relaxes, balances and stabilizes.

Transformation is an excellent blend for anyone who wants to be empowered and to make positive changes to an old belief system that no longer serves you.

Serra Gold is for the heart. It assists with circulation, inflammation and cardiovascular support.

Ginkgo Biloba

Ginkgo is one of those herbal medicines that's been heavily researched using controlled clinical trials. It is believed that Ginkgo is one of the oldest species of tree in the world.

I won't travel without Ginkgo because it supports my circulatory system, keeps my memory sharp and helps me stay focused. Who in their mid-life and beyond wouldn't like that? Ginkgo has been used to effectively treat Alzheimer's, depression and impotence.

My friend Jamie's adult son returned to school for work-related reasons and said his anxiety disappeared because he used two Ginkgo capsules before each class. He bragged a bit and said, "Mom, it really helped me feel on top of my game."

We've all been there in our early 20s and 30s, and sometimes our 40s, but it's pretty nice to feel that good in your 50s and beyond. Give *your* brain a boost and see what happens.

Essential Oils

The oils I recommend can be ordered from the website www.YoungLivingEssentialOils.com (as long as you use the one with oils with an "s." The grounding oil may be ordered off of this website.) If you want the oils wholesale, just get the $40 START LIVING kit, which has FREE lavender oil and peppermint oil in it and a 50% off diffuser coupon (which makes the kit free) and entitles you to get your oils wholesale forever, with no minimums ever.

My friends Dr. Julie and Gregory Montgomery teach classes using the oils in hands on healing. They love to empower people to take charge of their own lives and their animals lives as well!

They work a lot with animals and are the only husband and wife team I am aware of who do this type of work with both humans

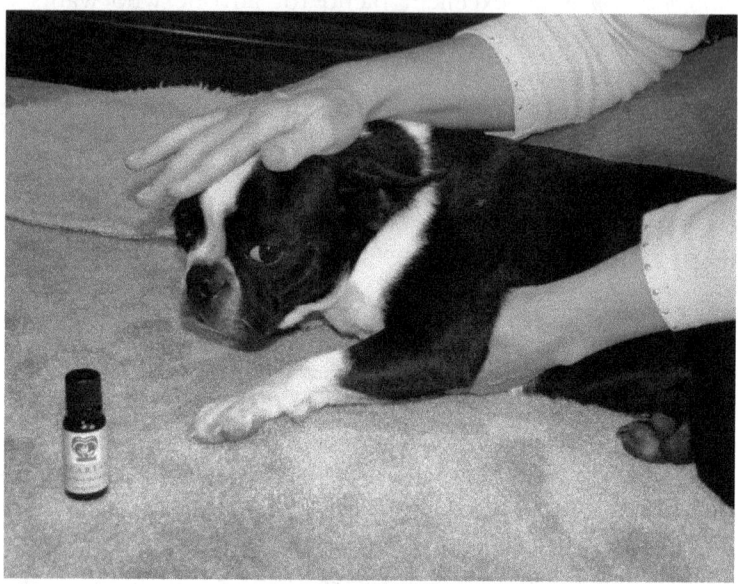

Dr. Julie Montgomery working with oils on a canine client

and animals. They especially love to work with horses and their riders. They created a healing modality called Quantum Relief, which brings balance to your energetic field and helps you help your body to restore itself to good health. This work integrates acupuncture, essential oils on meridians, aromatherapy, auricular therapy, herbology, homeopathy, naturopathic "water cure," polarity therapy, reflexology and nutrition. Go to their websites to find a practitioner near you.

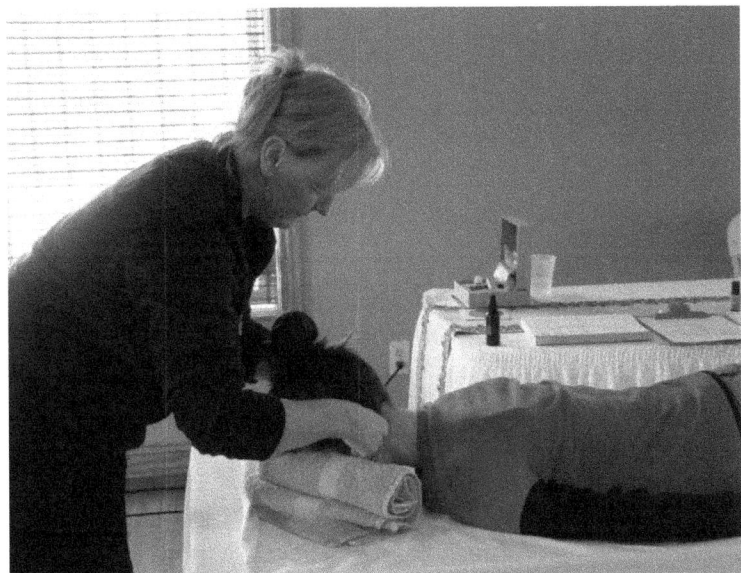

My friend Chris working with essential oils on a human client

Vitamins

"Good health doesn't have to cost a lot of money, but there will be some discipline involved."

Here's a short list of a few vitamins and their importance and usage.

Vitamin A is an antioxidant that helps to protect our cells against cancer and other diseases. Do not take large doses without proper supervision.

Vitamin B-complex is our nerve food. It's very important for keeping stress away by calming our nervous system, along with promoting emotional and mental stability.

Vitamin C is good for the common cold but also supports our adrenals during times of stress. It is excellent for removing toxins and excess water – very good news for weight watchers.

Vitamin D is absorbed through sunlight and food sources. It's the feel good vitamin, and comes from the ultra-violet rays we folk in sunny climates take for granted. Interestingly, many of my friends who relocated to Seattle, WA and surrounding areas became very depressed, and overly tired from a lack of having sunny days. Their doctors put them on high doses of Vitamin D and it worked.

Vitamin E is where we get our baby soft skin and shiny hair from. It's better when taken with zinc. Vitamin E is good for circulation, blood clotting, healthy breasts and PMS. It also assists in healing scars and leg cramps.

Calcium helps maintain healthy teeth and bones.

Chromium metabolizes sugar which helps hypoglycemia and diabetes.

Iron is good for preventing anemia.

Iodine influences the thyroid.

Magnesium helps convert blood sugar into energy.

Potassium supports our muscles and stops them from becoming weak. It also regulates the heart's rhythm.

There is a problem common to many women going through 'The Change.' A number of women have pain during intercourse, to the point of not wanting to be touched again. This feeling has much to do with the thinning of the vaginal walls and other factors, but the one thing that has helped me and other women instantly has been an herb called Raw Thyroid. It seems to work wonders and is used widely among chiropractors, and holistic and naturopathic doctors. Have your thyroid checked ASAP if you're feeling uncomfortable down yonder.

Your local health food store will carry kelp along with raw thyroid. Both have been beneficial to women wishing to enjoy sex again.

For more amazing information about vitamins and healthy living, please read Dr. David G. Williams' *Unabridged Library of Medical Lies* in which he offers:

> Myth #21: Nutritional supplements interfere with conventional cancer treatments.
> — www.DrDavidWilliams.com

Have fun, do a google search for doctors in your local area that offer Alternative healing for hormone balancing. Some local health food stores keep a list of doctors that practice natural medicine.

Vitamins for Our Children

It would be a sin against Mother Mary, Mother Earth and God if we didn't stress the importance of supplementing our children's diets with vitamins and minerals. Why? Because our society thinks it's okay for 7, 8 and 9 year olds and teenagers to be placed on prescription drugs – something absolutely unheard of fifty years ago, and looking at the results, this is not proven to be in the best interest of children in the long run.

Sure, fast foods are plentiful but not nourishing for the growth of children's bodies or brains. There are more dyslexic, bi-polar, autistic and obese children in America now than any other time in the history of our great nation. According to the Mayo Clinic, childhood obesity occurs when a child is well above the normal weight for his or her age and height. Childhood obesity is particularly troubling because the extra pounds often start children on the path to health problems that were once confined to adults, such as diabetes, high blood pressure and high cholesterol. Childhood obesity can also lead to poor self-esteem and depression.

One of the best strategies to reduce childhood obesity is to improve the diet and exercise habits of your entire family. Treating and preventing childhood obesity helps protect the health of your child now and in the future. So it's time for parents to take matters into their own hands by adding not only organic fruits and vegetables to the table every day but also vitamin supplements.

From Michael's Naturopathic publication, "Children are like gardens; providing good nutritional supplements today yields a healthier child tomorrow." However, be aware that not all children's vitamins are the same and most of those you see advertised on T.V. are packed with unhealthy amounts of sugar, as are the majority of store-bought brands. Michael's brands found in health food stores do not use added sugars in any of their children's products; they use xylitol, glycerin, natural juices and Stevia.

Michael's has a liquid multi-vitamin, Pedia Vites, for nourishing your newborn through toddlers. Also, their Children's Chewables for young children taste good and support good dental health. They also offer Pre-teens' and Teens' multi-vitamin tabs for boys and girls (gender and age-specific for different stages of growth) plus Boys and Girls Minerals that are needed for overall development of healthy skin, teeth and bones, while supporting restful sleep and reduced stress.

With today's hectic lifestyle of school, sports and the overload of distractions, it behooves us to give our children all the help we can in the healthiest way possible. Our family has used Michael's products for years.

For information, visit www.michaelshealth.com, or call them at: 800/845-2730.

Sugar Substitutes

Awareness gives us the power to help not only our children but also our elderly and ourselves. I'm adding this information just to tweak your curiosity enough for you to delve deeper for your own understanding about the current 'sugar-free' craze.

Have you noticed that we often do something to protect our children, and sometimes our animals more quickly than we do to help ourselves? Isn't that something for us all to ponder?

Earlier I pointed out that one of the sweeteners used in Michael's vitamins for kids is Stevia. This is a natural herbal sweetener from South America that has excellent properties and doesn't adversely affect blood-glucose levels. Furthermore, it's safe for use by diabetics.

On the other hand, many other products we let children consume everyday such as in diet soft drinks, NutraSweet, Equal, chewing gum, some yogurts and a plethora of other foods use Aspartame. According to the website www.dorway.com, the first carbonated beverages containing aspartame were sold for public consumption in Fall 1982, and from 1983 to 1990, there was a 67 percent increase in brain tumors in people over 65 years old and a 10 percent increase in all age groups. The greatest increase started four years after the FDA's approval of aspartame.

A special report by the Feingold Association about Aspartame says it has been associated with hyperactivity, irritability, aggression, concentration problems, and even brain tumors. Says Jane Hersey, the Association's Director, "The FDA has received thousands of reports of adverse reactions to Aspartame." The most frequent complaint attributed to Aspartame use is migraine headaches.

The report also looks into the other substitutes. Take a look also at Splenda (Sucralose), which is made by treating sugar with chlorine. And what about Sweet 'n Low, or Saccharin? The National Cancer Institute has evidence that 'suggests' heavy saccharin users may increase risk of bladder cancer. And don't forget High Fructose Corn Syrup, most commonly found in fruit drinks. Again according to Jane Hersey, some of the side-effects of (HFCS) are "Loss of iron and magnesium, and it may contribute to childhood diabetes."

From the American Journal of Clinical Nutrition: "HFCS in beverages may play a role in the epidemic of obesity." Hersey's suggestion for people who may be nervous about synthetic sweeteners is to use Stevia, honey, molasses and pure maple syrup.

Here are the symptoms attributed to Aspartame in complaints reported to the Department of Health and Human Services by April 20, 1995 (from an official FDA Document):

Reported Symptom	No. Complaints	% of Reports
Headaches	1847	21.1%
Dizziness	735	11.2%
Mood Changes	656	10.0%
Vomiting/Nausea	647	9.8%
Abdominal Pain	483	6.5%
Change in Vision	362	5.5%
Diarrhea	330	5.0%
Seizures/Convulsions	290	4.4%
Memory Loss	255	3.9%
Fatigue/Weakness	242	3.7%
Other Neurological	230	3.5%
Rash	226	3.4%
Sleep Problems	201	3.1%
Hives	191	2.9%
Change in Heart Rate	185	2.8%
Itching	175	2.7%
Gran Mal Seizures	174	2.6%
Numbness/Tingling	172	2.6%
Local Swelling	114	1.7%
Difficulty Breathing	112	1.7%
Oral Sensory Changes	108	1.4%
Menstrual Changes	107	1.1%
Symptoms reported by less than 100 complaints	1812	

Please feel free to read more with due diligence at: www.dorway.com. We can be the bridge for future and past generations to live healthier, happier and longer lives. We owe this to our children, our aging parents and ourselves. As Oprah says, "We can be the change we want to see."

Colostrum: the Immune System's Best Friend

Colostrum is good for supporting our immune systems and it supports the immune cells of the gastrointestinal tract. This is a biggie because many of our illnesses start in the gastrointestinal tract.

The two main components in colostrum are immune factors and growth factors. It is the first milk of all mammals, the immune residue of the mother, with immunoglobulins and other memory cells to keep newborns healthy during their first few days of life.

Colostrum, my friends, is a food not a drug. This puts a spin on the importance of women taking care of themselves during pregnancy and afterwards, especially during the breastfeeding process. Just remember that your emotional state is as important as your physical state, so do some self-nurturing at this time so you and your child will benefit and bond.

You have probably heard about how healthy 'mother's milk' is for her newborn baby. The mother, with all her protective antibodies, passes on her immunity to her baby through breast feeding. When a baby has not had mother's breast milk, it takes the baby about one month to develop its own immune system. During that month, if the baby gets sick, then some immunity might never develop because the immune system was so overwhelmed by some invading bug.

All mothers should understand that they give immunity to their new-born baby by breast feeding. A mother breast-feeding her baby is the only way it was done thousands of years ago. For millennia, there was no such thing as a bottle-fed baby! Then, the medical world changed. We went through a period when even physicians were telling new mothers: "Don't breast feed!" Now we know better. All the immunity within the mother is transferred to the baby through her breast-feeding milk.

When a baby was not breast-fed, researchers would find almost zero antibodies in the baby. Those antibodies were *not* there, and that baby was at risk. When a baby was breast-fed, the antibodies were there. A newborn baby has no antibodies - but within a few days on breast milk, the baby suddenly has a fully functioning immune system!

In the *Annals of the New York Academy of Sciences*, Dr. Brandtzaeg writes: "Antibodies in bovine colostrums are able to neutralize the most harmful bacteria, viruses, and yeast." A few more benefits are that it:

- Boosts natural resistance to illnesses and disease.
- Builds muscle mass and burns fat.
- Increases energy and vitality.
- Slows down the aging process.

More information on colostrum is supported by a large data base of clinical observations. Read more about it at your local health food store in the reference guide, or just Google 'colostrum.' Enjoy this food for the gut.

Collagen for Beautiful Skin from the Inside Out

We already know the wonderful benefits that vitamin E has for the skin orally and topically. So let's add more fuel to the fire and take a look at something a little extra. It's called collagen and it teams up with keratin to give our skin strength, flexibility and suppleness ... and that's a good thing, especially for us women, and given the ravages of pollution in the atmosphere.

About one quarter of all of the protein in your body is collagen. Collagen is a major structural protein, forming molecular cables that strengthen the tendons and vast, resilient sheets that support the skin and internal organs. Collagen provides structure to our bodies, protecting and supporting the softer tissues and connecting them with the skeleton. So it's literally the glue that holds together our cartilage, tendons and everything else that needs to be held together. At the same time, it firms our skin and improves our elasticity. Gotta love that!

The problem is, of course, that as we age, we no longer produce large amounts of collagen as we did in our young and tender years ... which is where collagen creams, powders, capsules and liquids come in. They are supposed to be the precursor to boost the collagen our body already has, and from personal experience, trust me, they work. I've had good luck over the years with the powders and the capsules so I'll keep on using them whenever I sense the need to firm things up from the top down. After only about three day's usage, I notice a difference in the firmness of my skin ... and I like that, as will you.

Firm and soft are good things, just like yin and yang.

Arbonne's Hybrids

Let's look at a complete vitamin and mineral package for both men and women, because we need more support at this stage in our lives. Arbonne makes a daily power pack combination of multivitamin and multimineral tablets, with calcium for bone support, antioxidants and digestive enzymes that work synergistically to address women's and men's specific health concerns.

Guys and gals, you will feel amazing and appreciate the am/pm pre-packs for your convenience twice daily. In this day and age of over-polluting our bodies, we need all the help we can get. My dentist said, "Since you've been on these vitamins, your gums have improved dramatically. No more bleeding gums and your gums have tightened up again with no more bone loss."

And my holistic doctor told me to keep taking them because they offer a complete program.

Contact a local Arbonne representative for more information.

Cranberry Capsules, Acidophilus and Enzymes
Tools for dealing with COVID-19.

We may never know the full scope of this Covid-19 pandemic, but we are forced to deal with it. This uncertainty keeps our bodies in a state of fight or flight (high state of stress) or fear of the unknown, which is dangerous for our overall health.

Some of the natural things we can do are to start with our nutrition and make sure we are eating fruits and vegetables on a daily basis. Along with incorporating good vitamins & minerals to ensure that we are getting all the necessary nutrients our bodies require for maintenance and repair.

For extra protection and prevention, my healthcare practitioner suggested the following:

- L-glutamine supports your immune system and other essential processes in the body during stress. It also strengthens your gut lining, which protects you from leaky gut.
- Olive leaf acts as a natural antibiotic.
- Zinc protects your cells.
- The Wellness Formula has 18 herbs that can fight off a cold or flu, if you start using it as soon as you feel any symptoms. This should be in every household for prevention.

One of the healthiest things we can do is to drink a 16% glass of celery juice each morning. Here are just a few of the benefits: It's packed with powerful cancer-fighting anti-oxidants, and it's a natural anti-inflammatory which contains Polyacetylene that helps reduce joint pain, gout, and rheumatoid arthritis. Celery juice also heals and activates the gut by restoring hydrochloric acid, which helps to digest our food better. It aids our liver, lowers cholesterol, lowers blood pressure, and is highly alkalizing. An alkaline diet can help prevent diseases.

If this lockdown has stopped you from exercising or you feel stuck and can't get motivated to make the necessary changes that will support you emotionally, physically, financially, or spiritually, then now is a great time to have your hormones checked. Your adrenals could be in over-drive, your testosterone both for males and females might be so low you can't start a task or complete them, or you feel overwhelmed or procrastinate. Any of these symptoms could mean it's time to get the hormones back in alignment. Check with your local health care practitioner.

My contact in Tustin CA is Dr. German Zermeno.(657)231-6164 He practices Integrative Medicine & Functional Medicine. One of my clients went to see him because she felt stuck and unmotivated. Her testosterone was supposed to be at 40, but it was at 4. After seeing Dr. Zermeno, she is back to moving forward with new business plans and has stepped back into the game of life with more energy and no hesitation. For me personally, my adrenals were in overdrive, and I was put on an herbal formula that has me feeling more in the flow with less stress.

We don't know what we don't know, but we do know that this Covid-19 is still here. It's up to us to be proactive, take whatever necessary precautions we must, and get back in the game of living life on a higher level than before.

The Green Revolution – Wheatgrass/Green Drinks

The following information about wheatgrass therapy was contributed by my friend Becky. It could impact the lives of you and your loved ones.

Many years ago, a woman inspired a new approach to healing that has remained an effective healing path for many. Ann Wigmore had learned secrets of natural healing from her grandmother in Lithuania. Her grandmother's use of greens and moss poultices and many other natural methods on wounded soldiers during WWI led Ann to create her wheatgrass cure. Wheatgrass is the result of sprouting the seeds of wheat and cutting the 'grass,' juicing it and drinking it regularly in small quantities.

After an accident in which 18-year-old Ann broke both her legs just above the ankles, gangrene set in and the well-meaning doctors of the time (this was in the early 1900s) planned to amputate. Drawing from her Lithuanian grandmother's knowledge, Ann refused the amputation, and instead had herself placed on the hospital lawn every day, to soak up the sun's healing rays. She ate the grass from around her chair and an uncle was able to bring her some edible flowers. In an amazing and almost unbelievable twist, a medical doctor passed by Ann one day and asked if he could take a tissue sample to his lab. He returned with the exciting results saying, "I think your legs are healing." They did heal and Ann had the full use of both her legs for the rest of her years.

Later in her life, Ann researched the kinds of grasses from all over the world and found that the sprouted wheatberry produced a superior grass. Using this finding, she started a handful of clinics where her grass therapy is practiced today, reversing cancers (including leukemia), tumors and other 'incurables,' and changing lives forever. People who have also been through chemotherapy and conventional treatments discover that, after learning the regimen of the wheatgrass and living foods diet, they no longer fear the recurrence of their ailment.

Ann Wigmore founded clinics in the following places: San Fidel,

NM, Puerto Rico, Palm Beach, FL, Lemon Grove, CA and a new one planned in Virginia.

See these sites: www.wigmore.org, www.optimumhealth.org.

Super Greens are good for us traveling people and people on the go who don't eat enough green vegetables, including a lot of the American population. Super Green powder mixes are high in antioxidants, which in turn support the immune system. The best green powder mixes normally have barley grass, probiotics, enzymes, chlorella and spirulina.

Drinking a glass of this powder daily is equivalent to 10 servings of fruits and vegetables, so don't underestimate how powerful these powders are and how important they are for your body.

In today's world when the fruits and vegetables from your local grocery store have been shipped from another state, sprayed with chemicals, and colored with preservatives unfit for cows, you don't know what you are really eating.

Reactions to Herbs

There are times when you're going through the healing process that you will add new herbs to your health regiment. For example when I'm home I juice vegetables to drink. One of my favorites consists of spinach, parsley and celery with a little lemon and ginger. It makes me feel alive, perky and ready to start my day.

Every week for at least three days straight, I'm on the road traveling and juicing is no longer an option. I tried several different green powered drinks and within fifteen minutes I would have an allergic reaction. This caused some irritation, to say the least, what was I to do? So I set an appointment with Dr. Devi and took a sample of the super green formula with me. She tested me for all the ingredients listed and found out I was allergic to the spirulina. This is very important to know because there will be times when your body's under stress and it starts fighting products that are actually good for it.

I went through a treatment for spirulina at Dr. Devi's office and 25 hours later, I was able to have my mix green powder without any negative reactions whatsoever. Think on this and don't get upset when a new product doesn't work for you. Learn to muscle test for products before purchasing them from the health food store. Go online and read the different ways to muscle test; this valuable tool can be used for prescription drugs, herbs, vitamins and yes, even people.

Don't just give up on finding new ways to heal yourself immediately. It took years for the imbalances to show up before I decided to do something about them, so don't expect to heal in two days. Falling back into old miserable ways of just popping a pill and going to sleep is no longer acceptable. No one will ever truly care as much about you as you.

The Nervous System

We have more options today than ever before to start healing our bodies and staying healthy and strong. It all begins with you. Something not to be overlooked while we're doing all this cleansing for our health is the nervous system itself. B-complex is wonderful for helping the body reduce stress and find a state of calmness.

We happen to live in a country where our diet consists of refined carbohydrates and processed foods that makes it easy to become deficient in B-vitamins. Hulls of grains have the highest amounts of essential vitamins, yet the hulls of grains are removed during the processing of foods.

Vitamin B1 and B6 are necessary for the production of GABA, the main calming neurotransmitter of the brain. As you can see, the B-vitamins play an important part in supporting us in our everyday stressful lives.

Along with B-complex vitamins, treat yourself nightly to a warm cup of Calm Powder magnesium citrate, known as the missing mineral. According to a study from Science Daily, "50% of the U.S. population is magnesium deficient."

When your levels of magnesium are deficient, this will affect the production of your energy and the workings of muscles and nerves. Thus muscle cramps may be a part of low magnesium along with chronic fatigue. Along with calming your nerves, magnesium has been known to help improve sleep, reduce the effect or frequency of migraine headaches, relieve stress, reduce pain, and promote heart health. Pick up a container or Calm Powder at any local health food store, and you'll notice a difference in about 2 to 3 weeks, if not sooner.

Dealing with Arthritis Naturally

There are at least 100 different disorders associated with arthritis. Some of these are chronic conditions that affect about 80% of all US adults over 65 years of age.

Something as simple as adding raw honey to your morning oats or tea is a great place to start, along with vitamin E oils. Spend some time at your local health food store, reading through the reference guide books there and speaking with the personal about other alternative approaches.

A few natural products that are commonly used include MSM, chondroitin sulfate, glucosamine and Sam-e. Remember not everything works for everyone and some medications counteract herbal formulas.

Chinese herbs not only help relieve pain but also calm the nervous system. Good acupuncture doctors are excellent resources. Always let them know if you're using prescription or over the counter drugs, what for, how many and how often.

Keep in mind that natural products work with the body's own chemistry.

Learn more from the *Nutrition Review* Research Update, vol. 5 # 2. Their information is priceless. Go to: www.nutritionreview.org/ and click on 'Subscribe' to start receiving their free newsletter.

The Aqua Chi Water Energy System:

Therapeutic Footspa - Healing for the entire family.

I spoke briefly on page 33 about my amazing energy healing experience years ago after using the Aqua Chi Foot bath. The first thing that happened was the shock of seeing the clear water turn brown with green around the edges while my feet were soaking. This made me know beyond a shadow of a doubt that those toxins were being removed from my body. That same day after the foot bath, I noticed how clear my thinking was and how much more energetic I felt. A week later, I decided to purchase the Aqua Chi Energy System for myself, my family and friends, and we were all in agreement that this has been one of the best health investments I have made.

Everyone in my family has noticed something different from aches and pains going away, to arm swelling going down, feeling much more calm, and sleeping better at night. By far, the most amazing experience I encountered was when I packed up my Aqua Chi System and took it to a nursing home to use on my friend Judy. After 15 minutes in the foot bath, Judy's skin started turning a soft pink, whereas before, she had almost lost all color and was looking a bit gray. I was certainly glad to see that happen. After 40 minutes of her feet soaking in the foot bath, her eyes were sparkling, she was laughing out loud, and her energy shifted right before our eyes. The staff members were so in awe and wanted to know where to experience it for themselves. I told them a few local places they could go to in the area and also to look online. The sessions run about $40.00 for 40 minutes. For my readers out there, here's a little more information about the Aqua Chi Water Energy System:

The Aqua Chi Bio Energetic foot bath combines the life giving properties of water with a specialized bio-electric charge, which enhances and amplifies the body's ability to heal. Some of the best results report:

- Reduced Pain
- Reduced Inflammation
- Improve Colon function
- Improve liver & kidney function
- Mental clarity

- Improve sleep patterns

If you are interested in learning more and buying this system for yourself and your family, please visit the link: htttps://aquachifootbath.com/?AFFID=465044

Lawyer talk: Please note: this product is not intended to diagnose, treat, cure, or prevent any disease.

Bone Health

Taking care of our bones in the second half of our lives is of vital importance. Osteoporosis is also referred to as a 'silent disease' so most people aren't even aware they have it unless a complete physical exam is done or a fracture occurs.

There are ways to prevent osteoporosis, and in earlier chapters, we've already shared the importance of well-rounded multi-vitamins, along with drinking plenty of good water.

Dr. Guy Abraham's study in 1990 suggested that 500mg of calcium and 600mg of magnesium have a significant effect on reversing post-menopausal bone loss within a short period, and that using those minerals increased bone density by 11%.

Vitamin D is beneficial in getting calcium absorbed into the small intestines and into the bloodstream. Zinc stimulates bone formation which in turn inhibits bone loss. Silica, silicon or horsetail (an herb we use for our hair and nails) help trigger the deposition of calcium phosphate, thus increasing the number of bonebuilding cells. Boron is a trace mineral that helps raise estrogen levels in the blood, and estrogen helps preserve bone.

If you like cabbage, that's a good thing because it ranks highest in its boron content. If you like avocado as much as I do, it's a good source of vitamin D and also helps turn calcium into bone. Avocados are also rich in vitamin E.

Folks, it's all about taking care of what we have been given, and the body beautiful and healthy bones go hand-in-hand.

CHAPTER SIX

Youth and Vitality - Hollywood's Best Kept Secret

Ladies and gents, when you look at some of our well-known actresses and actors and think, *She/he can't look that good and be 45, 50, or 60 years old*, in some cases, you're correct because plastic surgery is very common in Hollywood. In other cases that's not true.

While I was researching ways to improve my bone density, I happened upon a method for bone-restructuring called NeuroCranial Restructuring (NCR). It turned out to be the most powerful manipulation technique in existence. Developed by Dr. Dean Howell 25 years ago, this method creates permanent, incremental improvement in your structural alignment. This technique truly allows your body to return to its original design – your best-looking, most vibrant, harmonious, pain-free and energetic mode of functioning.

NCR can dramatically change your looks and your life in as little as 4 days. Here lies the gift: I was 49 years old, and my face was somehow looking flat, losing my cheekbones and looking tired most of the time. I was told NCR could help me with backache problems and to rebuild bones. I didn't know that a natural face lift would be part of the program – what a gift!

After my first 4-day session, I could feel my head and face restructuring itself while my head was on my pillow. It was amazing! A week later, the bones in my hands no longer hurt, the back pain was gone and I kept getting compliments about looking younger. I had no idea what people were talking about until I saw a picture of myself with friends. My cheekbones had returned, the bags under my eyes were gone and I looked vibrant again. I knew I felt that way but was surprised that I looked like I did ten years earlier. Wow! What a gift and how delightful this was!

I soon found out many celebrities use this method instead of plastic surgery because it's healthy and reasonably priced. Who would have known something like this existed and now the secret for healthy bones and youthful appearance is out. Dr. Howell travels the entire U.S. contact his office, tell Dr. Howell that Ella sent you.

Dr. Dean Howell 1-888-252-0411- they will gladly share a list of practitioners nationwide and globally that have been trained and certified by Dr. Howell. Youth and vitality is yours at any age!

Brain State Training – Another Best Kept Secret

Follow through, completion; you know those unfinished, aborted, artistic projects left undone? The book you planned on writing someday, the screenplay waiting to come out, the art work and the business you won't allow yourself to start. The procrastination stops here. Tax preparation used to take weeks and now it's only a few hours. Yes, it's possible even at 50 years plus to tune up the brainwaves.

Let's forget about all those dating services that promise the pie-in-the-sky soulmates. If you really want to upgrade the kind of men/women you've been attracting, then first and foremost stop wasting years on therapy and get training for your own brain. Yes, Brain State Training (known as My Brain Harmony) is truly the Law of Attraction on a higher turn of the spiral.

Brain State Training is for people who are tired of beating their heads against the wall and still haven't accomplished what they know in their hearts is possible for them in their personal and financial lives. Balance, people, is the name of the game.

Taking control of your emotional and mental state of mind – what a concept! Who would have thought that losing our memory would be a worry but we all know of someone who has.

" ... A balanced brain, harmonious life, healthy body and extraordinary result. There has never been more of a spoken truth. Brain harmony biofeedback takes a holistic approach to Neurofeedback, which helps the individual achieve higher levels of performance, creativity and happiness. This method is also used to help eliminate undesirable habits, issues or patterns."

— From My Brain Harmony

Myself, my friends and my colleagues have used Brain Harmony working with Jason in Newport Beach, CA. Our individual results have been amazing. I originally sought out this method to assist me in my research for a book about Feng Shui. At the time, I was busy in my Feng Shui business and wanted something simple for my clients to use if they moved furniture around or added new paintings, decorations, etc., after my initial consultation.

Two weeks after experiencing Brain Harmony treatments, I had a remarkable idea to produce a short film for my clients instead of a book. This project turned into a short, easy to follow DVD that would walk my clients through any room, home or office and show what the basic requirements would be to preset their spaces for balance. Again, knowing that an imbalanced home or office will impact your personal and financial life, it doesn't matter how beautiful or expensive your furniture is or isn't, because correct balancing is the order of the day.

I contacted a film crew through Chapman University, wrote a script and six weeks later, did the production for my DVD, *Simply Feng Shui*. Copies of my DVD were used as gifts for my clients, yet many people ended up purchasing them for friends and family. Using the skills I had acquired in harmonizing my brain, I attracted Diana Hull of Best DVD and Penny Wilton, a fantastic graphic artist who put my package together, using original artwork created by my son Luron (Maylay Sage) a graphic artist and hip hop artist. Their work together for my DVD and the outside packaging were superb.

Using Brain State Training gives you mental focus and clarity, along with control over your emotions to banish distracting thoughts that stop us or slow us down. I've seen this method help women who were desperately seeking men and consistently attracting unhealthy relationships, which is what happens when you come from an imbalanced state of neediness. Those women became so happy with their lives after using Brain State Training with Jason that they no longer needed a relationship to make them feel whole, because, of course, they now lived from a space of wholeness. Thus they began attracting healthier men like honeybees to flowers.

I've seen men who were good at their work become great at their work and attract more meaningful careers, plus have more balance in their homes with their wives and children. Some women have upgraded their business skills and redirected their life paths. These things are not to be taken lightly, especially when you're looking at people in their 50s, 60s and 70s who are benefiting from these changes.

Physically, the energy you put out after using Brain State Training becomes more of a flow. People with drug-related issues have been able to eliminate their addictions and completely tune into a new way of living. The people you attract to work with you on minor and major projects will amaze you. Because your brain is so synchronized with itself, it will easily support your forward movement. If you're really ready for a new breakthrough to new levels of achievement in your personal and professional lives, this method is for you.

In 2014, my beautiful mother, Mary Lucille Walker, died. I spent the last few months during her illness in Lexington Kentucky. I witnessed a family healing taking place as if by magic between different family members, a healing that was much needed.

After returning to California, I had a difficult time refocusing on my business. It felt like I had to work extra hard to get simple tasks done. I recognized the brain imbalance within myself and once again reached out for Brain State Training. Three years had passed since my last series of treatments. Jason was no longer in business, but I found an amazing woman from Awoken Life-"Mary McPherson." She added visualizations to my training that really kicked it up a notch for peak-performance.

The brain-map we did had shown the right and left sides of my brain working independently of each other instead of communicating. Similar to a male and female living in the same house, but speaking a different language.

It took more than a week for the treatments to kick in. The first thing I noticed was that my sleep was deeper and I felt refreshed the next morning. Then I was focusing easier on my tasks, researching the information for my new book, coaching my clients again with enthusiasm and back in the flow. I am so happy to have this technology available to share. Balanced brain, happy life, yeah.

My new contact: Mary C. McPherson- www.awokenlife.com
1-949-661-6909 - mary@awokenlife.com

Say hello from Ella, the author.

More Brain State Synchronizing – Fun, Fun, Fun!

After having a hard week, I decided I needed to be pampered before starting another work week. I wasn't sure what that would entail so I just thought about it like waves of water flowing by.

What would it be like to be nurtured? What would that feel like? So without another thought, I packed my bags for work. Knowing my layover as a flight attendant would be in San Francisco, I thought about going into the city, possibly having a massage, maybe going to a play and dinner. Just thoughts passing by. At some point during my flight, an older gentleman in first class who had been joking and laughing with me and others on board discovered we were all staying at the same hotel, so together, we all boarded the hotel bus at the San Francisco Airport. On the way, the same man received a call from the person he was meeting for dinner, telling him that the dinner meeting was canceled. Our first class passenger turned to me and said, "Would you and the other flight attendants care to join me downstairs for dinner? I hate to eat alone."

We all said, "Yes" because he'd been so nice and we were going to eat somewhere anyway.

When we arrived downstairs, our gentleman friend was waiting for us and ordered a bottle of Dom Perignon and, by the time dinner came, he'd ordered a second bottle and we were having the time of our lives listening to how this man had started his business on a shoestring, and now it's all over the world. The other girls told him I was celebrating my 50th birthday and he said, "Okay, then let's have fun."

He had the bellman order us a limo, and off we rode downtown with a third bottle of Dom Perignon to Ghirardelli's to have ice cream. When we stepped out of that limo in blue jeans and silk blouses, you'd have thought we were stars. It was truly a party.

While we were eating our ice cream, our friend took me back to the counter and bought each of us a gorgeous box of candy to take home to remember our celebration. By the time we ended laughing, eating, and having a series of delicious moments, he took me back to the counter and said, "We must buy some candy for each of you to take home for your Moms." Then he let me choose boxes of candy for the limo driver, the bellman, and the women at the front desk of the hotel. By the time we finished, I had a bag of beautifully boxed candies and felt like I was Santa's helper. Wow! All I remembered asking for on my 50th birthday was to be pampered, and my God, it kept showing up in the most magical ways!

We ended the evening back at the hotel, our gentleman friend hugged us all in the front lobby and said, "Ladies, I've got business meetings to prepare for and you have made my evening a day to remember." And off he went.

It was so magical that we all just looked at each other in awe. Most of this was due to the fact that I'd had Brain State Training earlier in the week to bring my brain back to its harmonizing state. Believe me, this stuff works mentally, emotionally and physically.

This is powerful work and you must experience it to know that the brain waves are hungry to be balanced and when they are, it's as if the brain recognizes itself again. And then you'll think a thought and it will manifest oh so beautifully before your eyes. You can dream your dream and watch it manifest in your new reality.

Some More Fun for Brain Harmony

Tony Buzan wrote a book, *How to Mind Map,* in which he helps you to use your mind creatively on paper to organize, plan and create new goals. This is a small, fun, easy book with 'show-and-tell' pictures.

Using a Mind Map is like drawing a tree and placing a theme in the center of it, such as 'my ideal future.' From there you draw the branches and make each branch a different color with a single word that pops into your mind as in travel, ambitions, exercise, employment and so on, bringing the right brain into action with the colors and curves. All words stem from the original concept of 'my ideal future.'

You're using branches on the tree and as the eye can see, there are no straight lines in nature. This is good because it opens the mind to continue to make connections. The larger branches connect to smaller branches as in travel can connect to a romantic weekend, a new lover, a new outfit, or even a new language. The curves of the branches really make it fun so you enjoy the process.

Of course, you can use a light bulb as your symbol and have new beginnings radiating from the central theme all around it, such as after a divorce, you might plan to go all the places your mate wasn't interested in and do things you put off or on hold. Yea.

Even though I've touched on Mind Mapping for fun stuff, it can also be used for note-taking, computer mind mapping as in sharing stored information and keeping track of projects as they move toward completion.

What about having an idea for a novel? You can plot main characters, the villain, the setting connecting the places and times where the events take place.

It really becomes fun for the brain because you begin seeing it as a whole instead of just sheets of paper you've written on and can't figure out how to connect them.

I have enjoyed Mind Mapping for years off and on for various reasons. Sometimes I just need to dream or foresee something completed. Sometimes I use it to see what new adventures would look and feel like as in a cruise connecting San Juan and St. Thomas – the food, the people, the dancing and the humming of the ship out to sea at night. When I allow myself to dream again, boredom goes out the window and joy steps in.

When you start using Tony's little book, home, family and friends and the events you do together become more alive. All because you threw caution to the wind, picked up some color markers or your kids' crayons and started mapping more ways to have fun and enjoy life. At the end of your life these bites and moments of joy are what you and others will remember. Enjoy.

The Internet offers many websites from which you can download free Brain Mapping software to run on your computer. The beauty of software over paper and pencil is that you can use your mouse to drag topics around in your map. Just Google on 'free brain mapping software.'

Brain Balancing Meditation: New Life

Visualize yourself walking through a beautiful lush garden of flowers of all colors with their own aromas – red roses, pink roses, white roses and even gardenias. Feel the breeze on your face and the birds singing all around you.

You see an opening. It looks appealing. It's a cave. Step into the cave. Speak your intent clearly. Place any obstacles that are in the way in a pink balloon and let them float away.

You're inside and you see stairs. It's dark but there are candles along the wall, so you just grab one.

The top of the stairs is step 30. Restate your intent. Slowly start to descend. When you reach step 15, restate your intent again. Continue your descent down to step 1. Give thanks for your manifestation and release it. "Thank you. Thank you.

Thank you. It is done."

Walk back up the stairs with a new stride and joyful anticipation.

When you reach the top step again, walk outside and let the sun warm your face and body. Breathe in the beauty that's surrounding you and walk out of your garden.

Look with wonder at that which is before you. Use any prayer or poem to stay centered and focused, and reconnect to your new intent.

Here's one of my favorites that Oprah used from Martin Luther King: "Use me, God; show me how to take who I am, who I want to be, and what I can do … and use me for a purpose greater than myself."

Silva Mind Centering Meditation

Are you looking to harness the full power of meditation in your life? I'm sure you're aware of the benefits of this time-tested and scientifically proven practice, yet maybe you've tried to meditate, but don't really understand it. Or maybe you've been doing meditation for years – but it's not as easy or effective as you want it to be."

Whichever of these categories you fall into, this is a very effective tool to experience a level of meditation that is deeper, calmer and more profound than you ever thought possible. Go the website www.silvaultramindsystem.com and download the free half-hour mp3 audio file.

Since the 1960s, Jose Silva has been developing and perfecting his mind training system. Over one million people have attended his seminars and his books have sold millions of copies.

The Silva UltraMind Seminar is the pinnacle of his work. Developed in the late 90s, just shortly before Mr. Silva passed away in 1999. Silva has always been ahead of his time. He was training people in meditation, self-hypnosis and creative visualization before these terms were in public consciousness.

Many programs offer affirmations, goal setting seminars, positive visualizations and meditation borrowed from Silva's work, but the Silva UltraMind System goes beyond this.

The Silva UltraMind System trains you to use your mind to such a powerful extent that within a few days, you are able to demonstrate ESP and influence healing in others. It also teaches you how to identify your mission in life and to use the power of your creative mind, to propel you toward this goal.

Health Today

In today's world it seems that people are finding themselves more overwhelmed than ever before. Life has only gotten more involved and complicated in the last decade. Thanks to GMO's in our food supply, along with the internet and nonstop communication devices, simple things like taking care of one's health can easily become a little more than an after-thought.

According to WebMD- "The US has the 7th highest CANCER rate in the world. Their Experts are saying lifestyle changes are needed to reduce the cancer rate."

They are blaming it on nutrition, being over-weight, over consuming alcohol and not engaging in enough physical activities.

What can we do?

From WebMD- "Getting more fruit and nuts, whole grains, vegetables, legumes, fish and eat less red meat."

I would take it a step further and say we need to eat organic foods, hormone free eggs, and hormone free meats. It's better to drink organic or almond milk, along with using herbs for both cleansing our systems and add supplements to replenish and rebuild our body temples.

Take some quiet time for yourself each day without TV's, phone's, computers or any other gadgets. Take slow deep breaths and sit to quiet your mind and just be, 10-15 minutes a day. Don't underestimate this simple yet powerful technique.

This life we've been given to live can only serve us if we honor it. I'm offering this information for us to live a balanced life in what many consider an unhealthy world. Look at your health today and begin now to make the changes that put you in charge of your life. Not tomorrow or next week start now, your precious life is in your hands.

FOREVER YOUNG

ELLA LADON CRONEY

CHAPTER SEVEN

Massage Therapy

Massage therapy is used for relaxation and reducing stress, and it rejuvenates and restores balance to our bodies. Massage helps with aches and pains, along with producing a calming effect for the long muscle groups and the entire nervous system.

Ladies and gents, there are few words to describe the power of touch (massage) on the human psyche! A dear friend of mine, Greg, broke up with his fiancée only a couple of weeks before the wedding. He was so on overload after this unexpected event that his friends suggested he get a massage just to calm him down.

Luckily Greg found a good massage therapist who was truly a gift. In his own words, as he lay on her table and she started to work with him, he began to cry. For the first time in his adult life, he was being nurtured by a woman without sex and it was okay. It was as if the therapist knew where to put extra pressure to help him release pent-up anger, frustration and stress.

Returning each week for a two-month period helped my friend get through his tough time and start to dream and live again. Old friends saw him and said, "My goodness, Greg, you look younger! What are you doing with yourself?" He just laughed it off but knew he had more bounce and vigor than he'd had in years. And for once he was happy with himself, separate from anyone else's 'should' or 'should not's. At some point thereafter, Greg noticed he was spending more time in bookstores and coffee shops and not missing the bar scene at all that he so dreaded re-entering after his breakup. He found himself having fun and easy conversations with interesting women and just enjoying the moment.

There is so much healing in touch and what a wonderful way to be good to yourself and allow stress to roll off of your body and out of your mind. Allow this gift in your life because, as adults, we're not used to having that wonderful touch unless it's when hugging children, family or friends. Certainly in this day and time, we don't get enough human touch. Why wait for a lover? Do this for yourself ... and your body will love you for it. Voila!

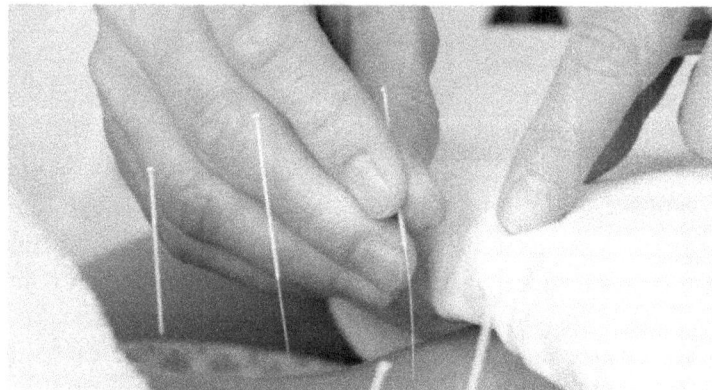

Acupuncture needles

Acupuncture

Acupuncture, an ancient alternative method for healing the body, uses ultra-fine needles inserted at specific points of the body to manipulate the central nervous system, which in turn improves our health and well-being. It is used in the same way that Feng Shui is used to balance the home environment.

Acupuncture doctors are aware of any nerves, tensions or organs being stimulated at any given point. Some doctors use heat lamps and others use a cupping method, which helps with circulation.

Acupuncture can be used for a variety of reasons including, but not limited to, muscle aches, back pain, shoulder pain, joint stiffness, (natural) facelifts, hormonal rebalancing and an overall feeling of well-being.

Check your local directory for the doctors nearest you.

In Orange County, CA, contact Dr. Henry Woo (714/5453181). Dr. Woo has assisted several of my Caucasian friends with natural facelifts.

In Los Alamitos, CA, contact Dr. Jean Fu (562/430-8889). Dr. Fu has assisted me and several pilots and flight attendants with neck tension, backaches, and hormonal rebalancing from emotional and mental stress, which can and will create havoc if ignored, causing costly problems later in the body/mind temple down the line.

A couple of days per week in Dr. Jean's office, we are blessed to consult with Dr.Wu, O.M.D., a college professor for over 30 years at South Baglo University/Zhijiang University of T.C.M. Dr. Wu is an amazing herbalist who mixes natural formulas from Traditional Chinese Medicines to aid the body temple in regulating and rebalancing itself. To say the least, my friends and co-workers are living proof that these methods work. If you find yourself in the southern CA area near the Long Beach airport, call and make an appointment with Tyler and experience Gina, Tom and Dr. Wu, along with Dr. Jean and all the different modalities that are offered.

Reiki

Reiki is another gentle yet powerful method for stress reduction and relaxation. It is a specific type of subtle energy work that is performed by a practitioner using the laying on of hands, allowing the flow of energy from the God Source to the client.

It is believed that this ancient healing modality brings balance to our auras and chakra systems. This in turn allows the body to heal itself emotionally, mentally, physically and spiritually.

Just a few of the benefits of Reiki healing are removal of energy blockages, breaking addictions, cleansing the body of toxins, pain relief, immune system support, and raising the body to a higher vibrational frequency, which in turn allows the body temple to heal itself.

Bill Diederich, a therapist and personal trainer, has been in the health care industry for over 30 years, and includes Reiki in his private studio along with neuromuscular therapy, pilates and massage. He has assisted fire and police agencies in L.A. and Orange County, and is heaven-sent for flight personnel and others who are exposed to unhealthy toxic environments.

Bill understands the body as a whole system (mind, body and spirit), and uses his expertise to help bring the body back to its natural state of harmony. Bill has helped many of his clients to get off of prescription drugs and their side-effects, teaching them how to move, live and work properly, creating optimal performance within their own body temples.

Feel free to call him at the Diederich Studio if you're in the Orange County or L.A. areas 949/697-8704 or drop an email to his office at diederich51@cox.net. Say hello from Ella.

I am now a Certified Holistic Life Coach and Reiki Master/teacher. Visit my website for more information www.ellacroney.com

Mastering Alchemy

This is an experiment for people who need to ground themselves and desire to know themselves deeply. For myself over the years, being a Gemini air sign and working as a flight attendant, I found it hard to ground myself before it was time to fly again. Even though I accomplished many goals I set out to achieve, there were others that stayed in my head and I wasn't able to hold onto them long enough for changes to take place.

There is an amazing workshop for people like me and maybe you, especially if you meditate. Visit www.MasteringAlchemy.com and listen to the free audio archives. These techniques offer one of the most powerful sets of tools for grounding your energy I've ever encountered.

The teacher of this work is Jim Self. He's truly on a path to serve humanity and prepare us for our next step in evolution. His free archives have essential tools that allow you to look at old, outdated situations, and have new insight as how to best change your life. Jim offers new ways to ask new questions to empower the thoughts you catch yourself thinking on a daily basis, thoughts that may no longer serve you, nor empower you mentally, emotionally or physically.

The weekend seminars are power-packed and Roxanne, Jim's partner, will help you state your intention to get the best out of the course for your growth. During the weekend, you will be given tools to take with you and use forever ... and we know forever is a very long time. Within days of completing the course with Jim, I had new career opportunities come available without my seeking. My work environment began to change right in front of my eyes, and it was and still is wonderful. These workshops assist us in blending the masculine and feminine aspects of ourselves, to live powerful lives and make wise choices. If you have a desire to outgrow yourself in style, this is the course to take.

Contact: Roxanne at 1-775/851-8950 or go to: www.MasteringAlchemy.com, and tell them Ella sent you.

DNA Healing – Clearing Internal Clutter

This information is geared toward people who've consciously been on their spiritual path and know something in life is holding them back from reaching their full potential.

People, it's time to wake up and look around you ... and notice with opened eyes and a clear mind how bombarded we are with negative energy. The T.V., the media, your family and your peers love giving you bad news or a lot of hype of which 95% is fear-based.

Unconsciously, we soak this misinformation into our world of thoughts and, in many cases, hold them there. We catch ourselves thinking unhealthy or negative thoughts that weren't even ours to begin with, but we allowed them into our homes and, like robots, we even have arguments over things that shouldn't warrant our attention.

This is where the DNA healings come in. The first thing you experience when working with Toby Alexander at www.DNAperfection.com is an Auric Clearing. This session cleans up your energy field on 15 levels of awareness, thus removing negative thought forms and negative energy patterns that can and do hold you back. What's happening is your light body is being scanned to have the negative thought forms removed.

If you know what it's like to have a heavy load lifted off your shoulders, this is exactly the feeling. You breathe deeply again and, as my friends and I experienced, new opportunities come to you as if a door to a magic kingdom has opened. It becomes easy to release emotional issues and some health issues start to correct themselves. In essence, your body is more balanced and you feel more at ease. "Peace be still" is the new order of the day.

Your next session is the Karmic Removal. It's time to let go of those old karmic contracts that no longer serve your higher purpose and continually cause disruptions in your life – drama, betrayal, loving someone but not truly loving yourself because the relationship is dysfunctional. You know about this stuff, such as being unhappy with the relationship choices you've made and continue to make, or making bad choices by attracting the same type of people, or staying in an unhealthy situation, be it mental, emotional or physical.

Women and men, it's time to grow yourselves up for your children and for the society in which you live. It's time to transmute the old baggage that no longer supports who you want to become, and to remove whatever's stopping you from going forward and living the life you promised yourself you would live, on your own terms, healthier and happier than ever before. We all deserve this.

The final two sessions are on DNA Healing, and with these processes, you take a giant leap forward spiritually and creatively. For myself and others, our creative lives began to flourish and we experienced much more joy without the drama. The funny thing about the drama is, when it showed up, it looked more like a movie outside of yourself that you happen to be watching. How powerful this feels as opposed to getting caught up in somebody else's show. Another side benefit in all of this is, the aging process slows down and you begin to fall in love with life again, as if the cells in your body remember the days of your youth. Yeah!

I received my training as a Golden DNA Facilitator, directly from Toby Alexander, and I now offer Auric clearings, which scan your light body, removes negative thought patterns- and other people's negative energy that can be holding you back from living an amazing life. Contact me at info@ellacroney.com for in-person or remote healing sessions.

Theta Healing and Coaching

This is an amazing healing technique you can be trained to do on yourself and others. It's taught by Vianna Stibal the founder and of course she has now trained teachers all over the world. In both of her books, *Go Up and Seek God* and *Go Up and Work With God*, she has DNA healing methods you can apply immediately.

In 1995, Vianna was diagnosed with bone cancer and, as the story goes, she went up to the creator commanded a healing on herself and it worked. Not only was she healed from the cancer but her right leg which had shrunken three inches shorter than her left leg, returned to its normal size.

In Vianna's revised and expanded version of her latest book, Theta Healing, she gladly shares miraculous healings from her clients and their stories. See www.thetahealing.com, 208/524-0808

HOLISTIC LIFE COACHING

At other times, you just need a coach to overcome-obstacles, become more organized, enhance self-esteem, or attract healthier relationships, and more abundance.

As a Holistic life Coach, I can assist you with these goals. Holistic is a form of coaching that represents the "whole", synergistic meaning is that the whole is greater than the sum of its parts.

Holistic life Coaching is dualistic in nature because it addresses the spiritual and physical aspects of a person.

Together we will work through a seven-step process to help you "reframe" the way you approach life for more positive and lasting outcomes. www.ellacroney.com

Change Your Encodements, Your DNA, Your Life!

This is the title of an amazing book by Cathy Chapman; it includes healing meditations using the Pillar of Light and my favorite – Accepting Michael's Sword. While reading this book by Cathy and Amma and using the techniques included, you begin to feel so loved and surrounded by light that an air of calmness comes over you. To say it's difficult to explain is true because you have to experience it to know it's real.

You will learn more about Amma, the great Mother, that loves you more than you will ever know and, with this wisdom, you become more trusting and more in tune with the world around you.

Together Cathy and Amma share information about a healthy balance between loving and being loved ... and who wouldn't want that? You will also learn how to live in love, about adventure and self-discovery and finally about the Encodement Technicians: Encodements are simply individual energy circuits that are connected together. It is fun practicing and activating the encodements to create harmony and new adventures in one's life.

People, places and events take on new meaning and life itself becomes more sacred. See www.lighttechnology.com and search on title or author to navigate to the book's page.

"Life is either a Daring Adventure or Nothing."
— Helen Keller

"Make the most of yourself, for that is all there is of you."
— Ralph Waldon Emerson

"Even if you're on the right track, you will get run over if you just sit there."
—Will Rogers

CHAPTER EIGHT

Balancing Your Home with Basic Feng Shui

Feng Shui literally means, "Free flowing wind and water." Keep this 4000-year-old traditional method simple. It's like balancing the opposites, male and female, day and night, cold and hot.

First, clear clutter. Wherever there's clutter in your home, it will eventually affect your body temple, your work, your love life, your money. It rings true to say your body temple can become more balanced and supported by balancing the energies in your home, because home is really where the heart is … or is not. Only you know this. There are many different forms of Feng Shui but this simple form is taken from the Black Sect Tantric Buddhist School, introduced to the United States by Professor Lin Yun. I had the honor of studying this sect with Nate Batoon in Anaheim, California at the Learning Light Foundation. I joyfully share it with you.

Feng Shui uses a small scale called a 'ba-gua.' The ba-gua has a shape very similar to our stop sign and each side of the ba-gua is significant. Everything works from the front entrance of your home, represented by the lowest side of the octagan shape. If your home is in a square, that's fine, as the ba-gua will fit inside of it. If not, just play 'Let's Pretend.' It still works.

Family Area: Green/Wood (left side middle)

If you're having drama in your family life, disruptions of peace, it would behoove you to look at this area. The Family Section of the ba-gua is to the left center wall or room as you enter the front door. If you have a T.V. there, watch out! You're inviting major drama, bad news and lies to your family life.

Heavy Wood supports this area, along with the Color Green. A healthy looking real or fake green plant will do miracles to support you here, along with family pictures preferably.

Wisdom/Skills/Knowledge Area: Blue Color (front entrance - left side)

Little wonder the Wisdom Area of the ba-gua is to the immediate left side as you enter your home. Support this area with the Color Blue and/or pictures or poems or prayers of wise saints or wise people you admire, and/or angels. Whatever grounds, the idea of wisdom for you should be represented near the entrance of your home.

The reason this area is so powerful is because it's directly in front of the family area and we don't always make good wise choices when it comes to our family. It's diagonal to the relationship area, and with the high divorce rate in our country, we can say again, we haven't made wise choices when it comes to our mating.

The wisdom area can certainly help rebalance all the areas of your home, including money, so treat this area as sacred, for it truly is. Think of the blue sky or the blue ocean, something expansive yet a part of everyday life, which we sometimes take for granted. Think of something soothing, and you'll move into this flow, becoming more thoughtful and more deliberate about the future choices you make concerning your life.

Helpful People/Travel Area Gray/Silver (front entrance - right side)

Directly across from the Wisdom Area still at the front entrance but on the right side, is your Helpful People Area. If you feel like nothing gets done unless you do it, then this is an area you need to spruce up. It's quite simple. Find the Color Gray, light or dark or a little silver box and place three requests at a time in areas of your life where you need assistance.

This section is excellent for a collage of travels to places you've been and places you wish to visit. You can sit in this area and contemplate unknown people helping you with a new business venture. They really do show up and, even a small, cute angel magnet on the fridge helps because you can't go wrong with angels on your side. No man or woman was ever meant to be an island. Slow down, work on this area, and stop going at it alone.

Health Area: Yellow (near the center of your home)

Yellow, like the golden sunshine, is our healing color. And just like the sun soothes, heals and warms us, adding the color yellow near the center of our home brings in the vibration of health.

The thing to do near the center of your home is to place a round, yellow piece of paper under furniture or hide it in a closet. Just like the sunshine, it's for healing the whole family and no one else knows it's there.

Creativity and Children Area: White/Metal (right side middle)

Maybe your children aren't doing well in school, or maybe there are no children in the home but the adults aren't creating new interesting or exciting life experiences. Maybe your life has become dull and mundane. The area of your home to bring passion back to life for creative projects would be the middle right wall, directly across from the Family Area of your home.

The Color White supports this area, along with the Metal element. Baby pictures and pictures of children playing are fabulous for this area. It's a great place for TV, stereo, books, school projects and computers. At the end of the day, leave crafts neatly placed in this area. If you don't have children in the home, find old pictures of yourself as a child. This will do wonders for your creativity. Remember, happy pictures of happy times.

Relationship Area Think Pink (back corner - right side)

Think pink and let's get down to the nitty gritty. Let's say your relationship is non-existent. It's as dead as a doorknob, and you're ready for a new one or you want to spruce up the old one. There's help on the way and this is by far my favorite area. In my consulting work, I've assisted women and men who haven't dated in years to attract amazing, interesting partners. So get ready for the juicy stuff.

The Relationship Area is the far right corner of your home or any room, assuming you're standing at the front entrance.

Think doubles for this area. A set of matching lovebirds, a matching set of wine glasses, and the matching towels you hang in the bathroom, two candles and the color pink help tremendously, even if hidden inside a picture. Use red if you need major help with your love life, as in two red identical candles. Also, on each side of the bed, have matching night stands.

Make a collage of happy couples doing the things you'd like to do, and place it someplace in this area. The collage doesn't have to be large but it should have couples wining and dining, or walking into an opera house, or on a boat, or out bike-riding. Just have fun with this. This is not the area for a picture of one person alone. No, not if you want a relationship in your life. If you're single but desire a relationship, do not sleep in a single bed, but use a double bed or larger. A single bed tells the environment there's only room for one.

For more intimacy, place a red sheet between the mattress and box spring. If there's no passion in your relationship, sprinkle red throughout the room as in the bed covering, in the pictures, red candles, a matching pair, of course, as red represents fire, but be careful as too much red is over-stimulating.

This is a delicate area. Please do not display pictures of friends with whom you have problems or negative family members or divorced couples. Keep this area for joyful times, joyful pictures.

Wealth Area/Show Me the Money, Honey: Color Purple (back wall - left side)

This is an amazing part of the ba-gua, in the far left corner of your home or room from the front entrance. Purple is the color here. Think royalty, think rich, and feel it. The Wealth Area is directly behind the Family Area, which means taking good care of the family first, for it sets the foundation for basic needs. Be aware that the Wealth Area adds all those extra joys of travel and other activities that require money flowing beyond the basics.

A water fountain in this area is amazing, or a picture of a boat coming into harbor as in, 'Your Ship Has Come In!' A round crystal is good in this area for balancing all that money that's sure to come in. You have to know what to do with it when it arrives. Have fun with this and add some pictures or a symbol that represents wealth to you. Please don't ignore the Wisdom Area at the front entrance because people don't always agree about money and it is smart to have more wisdom when it comes to spending, investing, and enjoying money. It's a make-or-break topic for many couples.

As soon as you decide to work on the Wealth Area, you should set aside some time to reevaluate your goals. This sets things in motion much more quickly and keeps things flowing smoothly.

"God's riches are flowing to me, like rain falls from the heavens,"
— Joseph Murphy

"Let there be peace within your walls and prosperity within your palaces."
— The Holy Bible

Career Area: Color Black (front - middle entrance)

The Career Area includes seeking a new job/career and/or creating a new business and or enhancing a business to grow. The color is black, the element is water, and having water near your front entrance creates very good chi. This is a great place to have business cards and/or affirmations hidden in this section to call in new clients, new work or just enhance the business you're already in. If you choose to enter a new vocation completely different from the work you're doing, place a book or reference information concerning the new vocation in the left corner – the Wisdom Skills and Knowledge Area – to support your new choice.

Fame and Reputation: Color Red (back middle-wall)

Head straight to the back wall directly opposite the Career Area for Fame and Reputation. The color is red and this area supports your reputation going out good and coming back good. It makes your word like gold. This is not the fake Hollywood fame of some entertainers who turn into horrible people as soon as the camera's off.

Find areas in your life where you truly want to make a difference and go after it. A red candle in this area will do fine, along with affirmations about how well you would like your business to be accepted by humanity at large. If your ideas are really good, other people as well as you will benefit. Life is all about balance and flow. Have fun with this.

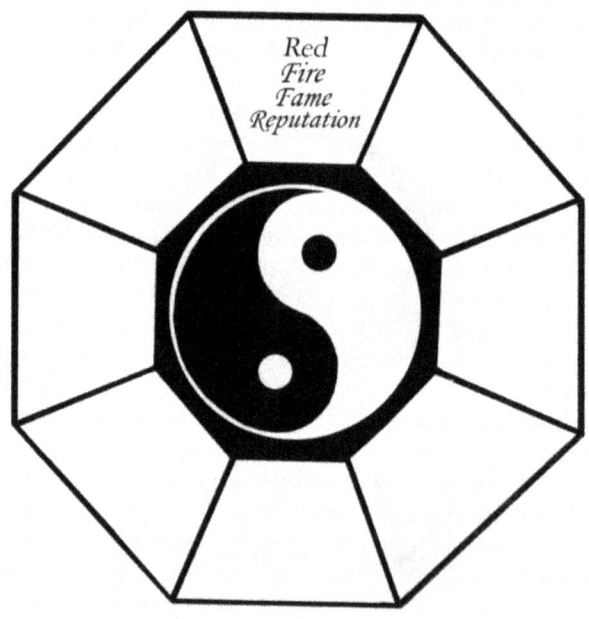

Testimonials

"What Ella has taught me through Feng Shui has changed my life and my family to a greater state of being. Her techniques of this ceremonial art bring her uniqueness of the craft. Each location I have moved to, Ella has shown me how to be more empowered, grounded and supported by Feng Shui in my own home. She's uplifting, and has fun helping others achieve their goals."

— Z. Chiess, Cypress, CA

Ella,
"We just got our new inventory load of 115 boxes of posters, and yes, we are flying! Thank you so much for coming over and helping us organize and clear out the energy in our house. Since we worked with you, we have sold over $20K this month in product sales! Literally the day after you were here, we sold 5 boxes of our product and it has not stopped yet! Thank you so much for your help. Your work is powerful and everybody on the planet should use your services. They will see immediate results!
Thank you!
With Love and Appreciation."

— Joshua, Cory's Posters

Ella,
"Thank you so much for the fantastic balance. I can feel the entrance way zinging when I walk in because of the wisdom and knowledge ba-gua on the wall. I can't wait to get more blue up there and really get going. You are amazing at what you do. I cannot thank you enough. Blessings always."

— E.Mahan eg@abbotkinneyrealestate.com

"Ella's insightful wisdom in interpreting Feng Shui principles gave me a creative approach and innovative ideas in applying these principles in my home. She has intrinsic ability to translate the art of Feng Shui for practical application with a soulful perspective."

— Kathleen Lowson - Founder of *Life Force Energy Institute and the Center for Peace*

Balancing Your Life with Spirituality

"Greater is he that is within me, than he who is in the world."
— Christ

Let's wake up! We were never meant to walk on this earth alone. Look at all the havoc in our nation, in the world, and now in our homes. Somewhere, somehow, we have forgotten basic truths.

I'm not preaching religion here, because religion has a way of excluding people. I'm speaking from a spiritual space of all-inclusiveness. I may not agree with your way of honoring God/Goddess but I allow it and respect it as what is right for you, knowing a universal truth that, in every language under the sun, mankind wants to love and be loved.

Take a step backwards in the last seven years in your life and find moments of joy, or peace, or harmony – something as simple as kissing your children goodbye as they run out the door for school, or shouting after them as they run for the door that you love them. You get the picture. Joy, as does love, needs to be practiced.

You can incorporate breathtaking moments in your life, like looking up at the millions of stars at night and being in awe that someone up there may be looking at you down here as a star planet and wondering what joy there is in beholding the gift of life down here.

Start asking questions, such as: "How can I leave this world better than I found it for our children and their children to come?" Including love with Divine Wisdom leaves us no choice but to make our lives more sacred and begin in ways, no matter how small, to acknowledge that ... and live it. If not now, when? If not you, who?

Stop sitting in the background, licking old wounds that suck the energy from your life. Stand up, pick up your own cross and carry it. Find out where or how you can be of assistance to others.

It doesn't matter how small a scale; it need not be grandiose. Just sometimes being present helps another, or perhaps recommending a new vitamin or herb that helped you in turn helps another. Or maybe just recommending a good CD. Share with them courses like *The Visioning Process* by Rev. Michael Bernard Beckwith from the spiritual center Agape. You saw him in the movie *The Secret* and on Oprah. I've joyfully shared his wisdom with others and it has proven to move their lives in a new direction as it did mine.

I happened to be in town for a Sunday service at Agape and an amazing guest speaker, Rev. Mary Manin Morrissey shared her personal story about being given only six months to live by the doctors when she was 18 years old. She shared how she chose life over death. Her book *Building Your Field of Dreams* is truly inspirational, and it gave me a new way to look at my life's work. You'll use it well.

Another well-kept secret for manifesting a well-balanced financial life is a book titled *Soul Currency: Investing your Inner Wealth for Fulfillment and Abundance* by Ernest D. Chu. This book will help shift your being into prosperity.

To those of you who are interested in beginning powerful meditations, let me suggest one of my favorite teachers, Georgia Lambert, who helped shape my life. Georgia is teaching *The Nature of the Soul* series online, along with many other amazing courses. If you are ready to take your spiritual growth to a new level, this is a great place to start. www.lambertslodge.com.

Don't be afraid to share the good news, since everyone else out there is passing out the bad news like jelly beans. You can be the change you want to see.

"I Praise my world as the perfect creation of Divine Substance. I now see more Health, Wealth, and Happiness in my world than I have seen before."

— Catherine Ponder, *The Millionaire from Nazareth*

Spirituality: Ho'oponopono

I once heard a doctor say, "If people were more forgiving of themselves and others, I'd be out of business." How sad but we know there's some truth to it. Personally, I noticed a few minor things in my awakening stages of growth that later led to 'ah-ha' moments down the line. And the changes started appearing when I begin using some transmutation techniques from my Nature of The Soul courses twenty years ago.

Releasing old drama re-runs, forgiving those people I thought had done me wrong (or made my life miserable) and letting go of the blame in turn freed up my energy and helped me create a new and more meaningful life of my own choosing.

I will be the last person to say it was easy but on some deep level, I knew it was necessary to let go of the old baggage. You best believe some of the old patterns have at times reared their ugly heads always in different looking packages. I would sometimes catch myself connecting this new situation to something old which I'd thought for sure was forgotten, but not so. Then I'd get busy and transmute again.

A few years ago, I found a great book called *Zero Limits* by Joe Vitale and Dr. Hew Len. In it is the ancient Hawaiian teaching of Ho'oponopono that involves four simple yet powerful phrases: "I Love You, I'm Sorry, Please forgive me, Thank you."

For myself and my friends who meditate, this has proven to be one of life's best kept secrets and now it's yours. Zero Limits is a must-read if you want to know what peace and forgiveness really feels like and how it transforms your life. The basic premise is that if you notice something out of balance in your environment, the fact that you noticed it means you are partly responsible for it being there and can be instrumental in releasing it. Ho'oponopono is defined as: "To put to rights; to put in order or shape, correct, revise, adjust, amend, regulate, arrange, rectify, tidy up, make orderly or neat." See www.zerolimits.com.

Flower Essences

Flowers! This precious planet is bejeweled with flowers. The gifts of flowers are not just in their beauty, but in their immense wisdom as well. If you love having the vibration of angels, the guardian, and creative, expressive, whole and balanced frequencies in your everyday life, you will love the flower essences.

Flower essences are, in my opinion, gifts of the spirit. They help heal your electrical, energetic system. The essence called 'Anxiety' is used to soothe the turmoil in your life, and thus you can see things clearly from a more balanced perspective. Using the essences named 'Jealousy,' 'Inner child,' and 'Neediness' can help get you out of a field of attracting unhealthy relationships.

The flower essences address your mental and emotional patterns; they are not a cure-all but they are powerful in at least lifting you from the depths of despair.

I have used these essences off and on for years with great success, and I love the fact that they are alcohol-free. You can put a drop on your wrist, place a few drops in a bottle of water and sip them throughout the day and/or place a few drops in your bath.

You will feel so connected and nurtured, especially using the affirmations in the free booklet that accompanies your order. Feeling and sensing the power and presence of your angels and guides is a beautiful way to live your life. If you believe, you shall receive.

For Flower Essence information, go to:
www.greenhopeessences.com, 603/469-3662

"Angels and guides are non-physical beings and spiritually evolved parts of you."

— Green Hope Farms

Drinking Water and Bath Soaks - Hydrate! Hydrate!

Healthy water is truly a priceless commodity. Third World countries' basic health issues could easily be taken care of if they had good drinking water and clean water for washing their clothes and for bathing. These are things we take for granted in our Western world but we shouldn't be so complacent. Why? With all our abundance, piped water, bottled water, drinking fountains, and all the reminders to stay hydrated, not all water we drink reaches our cellular level. We are not absorbing it! Most of the foods we eat are acidic and thus alkaline water helps us restore our pH balance.

There are so many brands of water that assist with better hydration, such as Pinta Water, Kangan water and a few others of good reputation. If you're lucky enough to live in or near Orange County CA, my friend Glenn at GC4 Health has an amazing setup of alkaline water you can purchase or a system you can use at home.

Remember, illnesses can't live in a body with proper oxygen, and good drinking water is a very basic start. Proper flushing of toxins and other chemicals you breathe in every day is essential.

Our water is truly a precious gift. The bodies we move around in and live in are made up of 75% water. The brain's function requires 85% of that intake alone to work properly.

Good water is the foundation for good health. Please treat yourself to a good read entitled *Your Body's Many Cries for Water* by Dr. F. Batmanghelidj because knowledge is empowering.

Note that not all bottled drinking water is the same. Most of the bottled waters are considered 'dead' because the minerals aren't there. From my research on what waters are out there, I have the following information to share:

Pristine Hydro Living Water sells healthy bottled water and machines, and believes water is the most important component for improving individual health.

From Pristine Hydro:

"Protect yourself and your loved ones from contaminants found in drinking water: acid rain, disinfection by-products, chemicals, insecticides, fertilizers, heavy metals, fluoride, and an array of pharmaceuticals including antibiotics, anti-convulsants, mood stabilizers, and sex hormones."

Safer Water, Better Health reported more than 3,500,000 people die every year from water-related diseases. Lack of safe water, sanitation and hygiene remains one of the world's most urgent health issues!

I personally have used Pristine water for over a year. I noticed a difference in my energy level immediately, along with no more constipation issues, and no longer dehydrated, just from drinking two glasses each morning.

Pristinehydro has added some other amazing products in their store. http://www.pristinehydro.com.

Here are two of my favorites, Shilajit, "the destroyer of weakness", and Antidote, "the most perfect food". Visit the site above and click on Pristine Nutrition for more options to living a healthier life with ease.

My friends Leslie and Tom ask me to try 9.5 Kangen water and I loved it. Got a boost of oxygen, was reading without glasses again, yeah. Now we have more healthy water options.

For more information please call 1 (949) 415-7017

I've also shared some life changing testimonials in my new book, www.amazon.com/dp/B013HIHZHW "HEALTHY TIPS ON THE RUN".

Do your own research; stay hydrated and stay healthy.

Bath Soaks

It's important and quite simple and inexpensive to use bath soaks for removing toxins and radiation.

> Bath Soak Recipe – these items are found at any local drug store:
> 1 small box of baking soda
> 2 cups of Epsom Salt

Pour the Epsom Salt and baking soda into a full bath tub and soak for at least 30 minutes. This bath helps pull radiation from the body because the skin is the largest organ of elimination. Bath soaks work wonders.

The most popular products for removing toxins and pulling excess sugar from your body, assisting it in rebalancing itself come from Miracle 2 N.O.W.

> 1 oz. of Miracle 2 Moisturizing Soap in bath
> 2 oz. of Neutralizer in bath

Again, soak 30 minutes.

Miracle 2 moisturizing soap helps remove dead skin and foreign materials. Miracle 2 Neutralizer helps detoxify your blood stream and create an alkaline condition.

Call JJ Lane to order and ask for the DVD on other products available and their use. 919/731-2355, www.miracle2angels.com.

The All American Diet and the Raw Family

There's a little book that can fit in your pocket called *Raw Family*. It's a true story of awakening and is a keeper. Some books you read and pass on to friends but not this one. This book will serve as a healthy reference for eating for the rest of your life.

I'm sharing bits and pieces of their story because I personally have known and still know families who have major health issues due to bad eating habits that are mislabeled as 'good.' The brain is a delicate organ and can easily be fooled into believing anything real or unreal, healthy or unhealthy. But the power of your will can help you take one small step to set you free on a road to recovery and loving life.

The book is about the Boutenkos, a beautiful Russian family sharing their experiences of living the American dream and nearly dying because of it. Starting with Victoria, the mother who, within two years of moving to the U.S., watched her weight shoot up to nearly 300 pounds. She joyfully shares how impressed she was entering a grocery store and seeing all the different colored boxed cereals and, of course, she had to try them all. Then there was her first experience with Dunkin' Donuts, which wasn't much to speak or write home about and she couldn't understand the hoopla about them. So she went back and tried them again and by the third time, she was hooked. Brain messages tell your cells that this unhealthy situation, food etc., isn't really that bad. Sugar is a chemical that changes your brain wave patterns.

The mother soon developed serious health problems, like an unsteady heartbeat, numbness in her left arm and depression, all along with the excessive weight gain. Just like the cold or flu runs through a family, so does ill health. And in most cases, mothers get the medicines or herbs, etc., make doctor's appointments, and do whatever it takes to get the family back on track. As I've said before, women are the glue that holds the family together, and it's time to honor that.

Victoria's daughter had asthma and thought it was normal. Her son had mood swings and a really bad temper, along with juvenile diabetes. Her husband had shaky hands, was extremely irritable, and had hyperthyroidism with arthritis. I'm just touching on what they went through, and ... wait until you read their entire story – it will be your wake-up call if you've been ignoring any of these symptoms in your family's life.

None of this should be taken lightly but here in the U.S., we're so used to Band-Aid treatments, the latest Hollywood diet, and the latest diet-pill, and wonder why our children are among the unhealthiest in the world. Duh. It's time to pull the covers back, get out of bed, and ask what is really happening here.

Well, Victoria took matters into her own hands, reading and researching, and asking strangers who she thought looked vibrant and healthy, "What are you doing to look that way?" She learned about alternative ways to help her son because she wasn't going to make him a victim to insulin shots for the rest of his life, even though the doctor said, "You have no choice and I'll report you to Family Services for putting your son in danger by not giving him insulin." Victoria knew in her heart and with every fiber of her being because she had given birth to this child that the doctor's decision was not a good choice for her son, and by the grace and power of God within her, she would find another way ... and she did.

Do not give your power away to the FDA, a doctor, a man, a woman, your Government or anyone that tells you, "You have no choice." As long as you have breath, you have a choice. As long as you have half a brain, you can engage it and find another way to make life work for you. As long as you can think, you can tune into the power within you and make a way out of no way. This is the free will promised to us all, and now is the time to start using it. Please read the book Raw Family, and get inspired. The recipes included are delicious and easy to prepare. Visit www.RawFamily.com and sign up for their newsletter. Or email: Victoria@rawfamily.com.

When Air Travel Hits a Bump in the Road

I must first say how grateful I am to have had a career with the airlines for twenty years now. I have an extended family of crew members, and I've enjoyed meeting people from all over the world and visiting places I'm sure I wouldn't have considered going to before my flight career. The freedom, the frills, and the thrills are real and I have enjoyed them and then some.

It wouldn't be fair or truthful to say, however, that this career didn't come with a price. That price for me was a toxic poisoning incident from breathing bad air about eight years ago, which in turn forced me to use these alternative health methods I've shared with many colleagues and with you in this book.

As I said in a previous chapter, after having my toxic incident and ending up in the emergency room along with expensive and extensive tests, the doctors still weren't able to help me or pinpoint what had happened to me. Luckily or blessed or both, I had Dr. Eberle and Dr. Previtera to turn to because they both knew about toxins and how to test for them.

After having hair, blood and urine analyses done, the lab report came back and said I must work in a chemical plant or on or around airplanes. The list of toxins found in my body filled five pages. My doctors grounded me for three weeks and put me on herbal formulas and high colonics to detoxify my body and regain my health.

I share this information with you because airline crew members aren't the only ones affected by bad air quality, toxic fumes, bleed oil leaks (cabins are pressurized by drawing 'bleed air' from the engines) and OP (organophosphates in the engine oil) poisoning. It sometimes happens to flying passengers after a flight who get misdiagnosed by their conventional doctors. Symptoms may be acute, i.e., for a short time after a flight, or chronic, i.e., long-lasting. Any of the following may be experienced: fatigue – feeling exhausted even after sleep, blurred or tunnel vision, shaking and tremors, loss of balance and vertigo, seizures, memory impairment, headaches, tinnitus (ringing in the ears), light-headedness, dizziness, confusion /cognitive problems, feeling intoxicated, nausea, diarrhea, vomiting, coughs, breathing difficulties (shortness of breath), tightness in the chest, respiratory failure requiring oxygen, increased heart rate and palpitations, and irritation of the eyes, nose and upper airways.

I'm not telling you this to make you afraid but to make you aware. I personally know crew members and passengers worldwide who were forced to leave their careers because of memory problems, chronic fatigue and neurological problems, along with MS and nervous system disorders. This, my dear ones, is nothing to shake a stick at and wish it would go away.

I am asking you to please educate yourself. Go to www.aerotoxic.org to read about Captain John Hoyte's experiences, his articles, testimonials and evidence that toxic exposure is real. Together, we can get governments to support the airlines and make the sky friendly enough and safe enough for everyone to travel. We must fit toxic fume detectors, filter bleed air and remove OPs from jet engine oil. Contact Captain John at info@aerotoxic.org.

> "If you think you're too small to have an impact, try going to bed with a mosquito."
> — Anita Roddick

Holistic and Naturopath Doctors

I have found many people over the years who are afraid of stepping outside of their comfort zone to look for new doctors. Here's a bit of information to assist.

Just like medical doctors, holistic doctors hold a medical degree but adhere to alternative methods first to promote physical, emotional and spiritual health. The use of prescription drugs is a last resort but can be done when necessary. Holistic healing synthesizes the wisdom from different health care modalities and cultures by treating the whole persona.

Naturopath doctors study 4 to 7 years and are educated in the same basic sciences as an M.D. but they also study holistic and non-toxic approaches to healing. Naturopathic doctors work on disease prevention, homeopathic medicine and nutrition to find a pathway to natural health.

For more information regarding Holistic and Naturopath doctors do a Google search doctors in your area.

"Always Do Your Best. Your best is going to change from moment to moment; it will be different when you are healthy as opposed to sick. Under any circumstance, simply do your best, and you will avoid self-judgement, self-abuse and regret."

-Don Miguel Ruiz

Nurturing for Spiritual Balance and Sanity

If women learn only one thing during their early years of marriage and child-rearing, that one thing which is often overlooked is taking care of yourself. As years go by and you get caught up in the home, furniture, shopping, parties and when to eat out, etc., somewhere deep down in the bag of chips, you'll ask where the hell are you? Or as a friend once said, all she wanted to do was take a bath or shave her legs without being interrupted.

We give, we share, we give more – that's just what we do. Sadly to say, many doctors of the Western world believe breast cancer is closely linked to long held resentments, suppressed emotions and not being fulfilled.

When it comes to nurturing, one of my favorite books I re-read at least twice a year is *A Woman's Worth* by Marianne Williamson. In the book, she speaks of a time in the distant past when the earth flourished. The feminine qualities of compassion, kindness, nurturing, generosity and non-violence were shared by both woman and men alike.

Can we dare believe that a healthy, balanced, harmonious world to live in could ever be even a remote possibility? Yes, because this is the stuff dreams are made of. This is why we pray and meditate for world peace, and we know it starts with us, in our homes with our families, and with ourselves.

We women are the glue that holds families and communities together. We are the gatherers, the nurturers – that's what we do. But in that gathering, we must not leave ourselves out of the equation. A little time set aside weekly for ourselves is not only necessary, it's essential to our well-being.

From *A Woman's Worth*:

"A woman is meant to hold the heart of the world within her hands. She must cater to it and minister to it and kiss it when it cries. We are meant to keep the home fires burning, the fires in our hearts. We are meant to prepare the food, the spiritual food of love and compassion."

Sorry ladies this cannot happen until we learn to replenish by being good to ourselves, loving ourselves and nurturing ourselves. We will, we can and we shall.

In Marianne's book, she goes on to say, "We are all sisters of a higher order."

Contemplate that, walk around with that, chew on it. It's high time for us to wake up and accept the power that flows through us to live a creative and purposeful life, to be all the good we can be, and be accountable for what we pass on to our children.

So we ask, what would that feel like, look like or how it will show up? It will be love under new management. Now meditate on that.

For more relationship information, please go to www.JimSelf.com. Have fun reading *A Woman's Worth* and enjoying Jim's courses. Tell him hello from Ella.

CHAPTER NINE

Deposits of Wealth

In 2007, I had the opportunity to visit the well-known Unity of Tustin Church, in Orange County, California. It was my first time going there and Jean Houston was presenting a two-day seminar called *The Mystery of Making a Difference.* Jean is an amazingly gifted story-teller/teacher, using ancient wisdom techniques and mythology for weaving a tapestry of possibilities for the future of humanity en masse.

Strangely, the morning before going to Jean's workshop, I had spent time outside among the lovely old trees near Nellie Gail Ranch in Orange County, California. I watched a couple of kids riding their horses, and mature couples strolling by, just taking in the beauty of a bright sunshiny day. The setting itself reminded me of my childhood back in Kentucky at Keenland Racetrack with my Dad and uncles, walking and feeding the horses and braiding their long tails.

Then a breeze left a scent in the air and my thoughts put me in my grandmother's kitchen early in the morning before anyone else woke up on Saturdays. I'd watch my grandmother moving around the stove, smell the Folgers coffee perking and listen to her singing. Those early morning memories of being at the race track with my Dad or being in the kitchen with my grandmother made me smile and I realized how rich my life has always been – from a space of wealth from the soul.

My Dad and uncles worked hard but laughed all along. My grandmother, no doubt, worked hard but sang all along about how lovely life can be from those simple pleasures. The very next moment, I was being pushed on a swing by my childhood friend Jeannie Morgan. My heart was so full of these little clips of life's joyful moments that, by the time I reached Jean Houston's workshop the next day, I was floating.

First, Jean asked us to participate in a right brain/left brain exercise: on the right side, see an eagle; on the left side, see a bouncing ball; on the right side, rock a baby; on the left side, eat an apple. This game went on for at least twenty minutes and we all had so much fun, we wanted more.

Later in the workshop, I mentioned to Jean that I had spent the previous morning recalling bits and pieces of my childhood and I called them my 'deposits of wealth,' like bank deposits from the Universe sharing its gifts of life's joyful experiences. Jean loved it and invited me to the front of the room with her and we shared more about this practice.

It's a blessing for me to now share with you the following exercise:

Take a walk somewhere outside in nature. How many clouds can you count floating by? How many stars can you count in the night sky? How many grains of sand can you count in your hand? It's all here for your enjoyment – the abundance of life. All there is to do is acknowledge it and breathe it in for the sacredness it is and the fullness thereof.

Allow yourself to own wealth from an entirely different perspective from the glamour we've been sold and mislead by. In Jean Houston's book *The Possible Human*, she has an exercise (#4) – a technique called 'Pleasure and Then Some.'

This technique grew out of an experiment Jean did with a group of her friends. She asked them to list their most pleasurable experiences and associations. Here are some examples from their lists:

1. Saturday afternoon movie with a giant Mr. Goodbar.
2. Hearing a choir rehearsal as I walked down the street.
3. Reading a great novel in a hot bath on a cold night.

You get the gist of it. Start now with your own deposits of wealth, listing five or so each night for a week or so ... and watch how magical your life becomes. By the way, on page 63 in the same book, Jean has that right brain/left brain exercise. It's fun to do with two or more – the larger the group, the more fun. It lifts everyone's vibration in the room and leaves you wanting more.

You're older now and hopefully wiser. Step back. Sit more in silence. Take a long look at your life and circumstances, and dare to pronounce everything sacred:

- "Treat the available people in your life as though they were the desired people.
- Treat the available circumstances as though they were the desired circumstances.
- Treat the available supply as though it were the desired supply.
- Begin now to praise and bless that which you have previously condemned.
- Adapt in this way to both the seen and the unseen good at hand.
- The desires of your heart begin to materialize more and more results.

"This is the Prosperity Law of Adaptability."
— From *The Millionaire from Nazareth* by Catherine Ponder

"While some of us were achieving comfortable homes and extensive travel to resorts around the world, we were also discovering that putting our physical worlds in order was only part of the challenge of mastering our survival. Along the way, we realized that our mental, emotional and spiritual natures were important ingredients to our long-range goals of survival, as well."
— From *Visionaries Thrive in All Times* by J. Hamilton

Any time when you're feeling down or your money's funny, these books, *The Possible Human* by Jean Houston and *The Millionaire from Nazareth* by Catharine Ponder, will get you back on track just in the nick of time. Start now.

Live, love, laugh, work and play with passion while calling forth new possibilities.

Healthy Living through Pain

It's highly unlikely for someone 50 years plus to not have experienced a major illness, divorce, financial disruption or death of a loved one. If you're the type of person who has no time to read but loves books on tape/CD/m3p,etc., a good starting point for you is Joseph Campbell's book, *A Hero with a Thousand Faces*.

This book on tape may be the prelude for many more to come. Why? Because it makes you contemplate the messages you've being given and their underlying meanings.

It's not enough to go through a divorce and look for someone else to replace the one you just walked or ran away from. Ask what happened up to this point that you didn't pay attention too and keep asking and diving deeper for answers that set you free, not just in body but the mind.

I've known women who have had three bouts with cancer. What did they ignore the first two times? What were they afraid to change that would have set their spirits free to soar?

Joseph Campbell says, "Myths are the dreams of the World." Sometimes it's easier to hear stories, yet myths are more than just stories for entertaining.

In his volume 1, he says, "These tales spring from roots of our consciousness. They transcend all boundaries, be they time, space or cultural. The hero/heroine is a metaphor for every individual's quest for fulfillment. Take yourself on this journey with Joseph Campbell and watch life reveal itself to you and you to it.

Read more at: www.josephcampbell.com.

Manifesting Before the Secret

Another of my favorite books I'd like to share with you is *Ask and It Is Given*, containing the teachings of Abraham by Esther and Jerry Hicks. Some of their amazing work was featured in the original version of the movie, *The Secret*.

This is a book I use when I want to dream again and call forth new adventures in my life. Have you noticed that as people get older, some of them stop dreaming but keep complaining that nothing changes or about how bad things are. Your life can change for the good and it doesn't matter what age you are, as long as you're still breathing, there's hope.

Page 109, Chapter 21, of *Ask and It Is Given* tells us that we are only between 17 and 68 seconds away from fulfillment. Now, wrap your mind around that. New manifestations can happen quickly but must be given undivided attention. "Within 17 seconds of focusing on something, a matching vibration becomes activated. If you manage to stay purely focused upon any thought a little longer, (hopefully a positive thought) for 68 seconds, the vibration is powerful enough that its manifestation begins." I love that.

We can easily learn new skills for retraining our minds and being in control of where we place our attention. How much time and attention do you give to the daily news via T.V., the Internet, or a newspaper? How much of that news is good? You get my drift.

This book and so many others are filled with wonderful techniques to assist you in becoming more conscious of the thoughts you're allowing in and around your environment. If you can't find anything to feel good about, if you're in an unhappy relationship, job etc., now is the time to do something about it. The Abraham teachings let us know that we have the power within us to create a magnificent life. Have fun with this.

For those who want to know more, there is a wonderful audio series offered titled: *Abraham Speaks through Esther Hicks*. I've had it so long it's in cassette form but yes, they now have them on CDs and m3p.

In the series, a few things offered are: the Law of Allowing, Bodily Conditions, Law of Deliberate Creation, Relationships and Agreements, Joyous Survival Christ Consciousness and much more.

Call 830/755-2299, and say hello from Ella, or visit:

www.abraham-hicks.com.

Abundance

The Abundance Book by John Randolph Price has been a part of my library for over twenty years. It was introduced to me by one of my favorite teachers, Carol Dore from her course on visualization.

Inside this little book is a 40-day Prosperity Plan that really opens you up for attracting more prosperity in your life from places you never thought of or dreamed of receiving anything from. For example, I've received checks in the mail from insurance agencies and mortgage companies I've overpaid, and unexpected gifts from loved ones, along with money in bank accounts I'd forgotten existed.

The book includes 10 abundance applications to meditate on daily, and you will go through the list four times each. If you use it the way the author tells you to, it really works.

There's information in this little book that I'd like to share which we may or may not have known before. For example, "The Emperor Theodosius made Christianity the sole and official religion of the state of Rome in 395. The institution assumed complete control over individual minds, and humanity entered the thousand-year period referred to as the Dark Ages. What is today 'prosperity consciousness,' – the realization of God as the Source of all good – was almost nonexistent."

This tells us how important it is to invoke the sacredness of God/Goddess/the Blue Virgin/The Light/Christ – or whatever works for you to rise above the old paradigm of separate religions into the spiritual space of all-inclusiveness, the One and the Many, the Many and the One.

This book will make you rethink how you look at abundance in your life in a most simple yet profound way so as to work with you, through you and for you, as does God.

A few examining questions from *The Abundance Book* are:

1. Have I totally surrendered all my needs, desires, fears and concerns to the Presence within?
2. Is my heart overflowing with Thankfulness and joy for the majority of my waking hours?
3. Am I listening to the Voice Within for guidance and instructions regarding any action I am to take in the outer world? Am I following through with action?
4. Where is your faith? Look around you. Your world simply reflects your faith.

There are more questions you'll read in John's little hand book. I personally have purchased at least ten copies of this book over the years and given them to friends and family. Two out of ten people read and used the methods inside and attracted amazing results in their lives, including new cars, new relationships, new homes, and new jobs just to name a few good things that have happened for them. The other eight or so are still complaining, blaming or looking for someone else to save them from their own miserable lives. You choose.

The Abundance Book by John Randolph Price is easy to find in any book store and, of course, through Amazon.

A Creative Lifestyle

Companies from all over the world are built around gaining and keeping our attention, because where we place our attention, we also place our time, energy and money.

Think on this. Millions, if not billions, of dollars are spent to find out where and how you live, and to hit you with advertisements via TV, magazines, newspapers and the Internet.

Wake up people! Not everything that is good *to* you is necessarily good *for* you.

Turn off the TV sometimes, limit your computer time, and invoke your creative power! Spend more time outside in nature, with your mind surrounded by beauty in museums, parks, by oceans, rivers or creeks. Find old books and new books that feed your mind with good stuff that trains your brain in a healthy way. Find books that inspire you to make small changes throughout your busy week. Study a new language; learn more about meditation and balancing the mind; take a yoga class for stretching and breathing. Learn how to create calmness that you can carry with you in the hustle and bustle of your busy life. Read more on nutrition, organic herbs food and vitamins.

The second half of your life is a great time to set new intentions and become the steward of your wandering mind that allows you to weed out 'microwave quick fixes' that have never and will never serve your highest good. Turn down the noise in your head and allow yourself to sit in quietness for five minutes each morning and evening, and contemplate and reflect on the changes that are necessary for you to begin living a whole, fulfilled, healthy happy and balanced life.

The only reason people become bored, fat and lazy is simply because they quit living a creative lifestyle. It's hard to live creatively when you're stuffing your mouth with bad foods – too many pastries, too much white flour and sugary substances. What brain can get past that? So your energy's sucked out of you and your senses are dulled, and you blame anything or anyone else for you not taking responsibility for you.

We are placed on this planet through the very act of creation itself – from above to below, from within to without. Creativity and creating shouldn't stop at any age. I'm hoping you will use this book to do whatever it takes to get your life back on track, and live the fabulous life you promised yourself you would live.

Life is for the living, the laughing and the loving. May you live in the magic of life.

My son, who is a graphic artist and musician, has inspired me to keep my creativity alive.

Vallecitos Mountain Ranch

"I went to the woods because I wished to live deliberately, to front only the essential facts of life, and see if I could learn what it had to teach, and not, when I came to die, discover that I had not lived."

— Henry David Thoreau

The Vallecitos Mountain Ranch is a wilderness ranch and contemplative center that supports and empowers you to be a strong and effective change maker and social entrepreneur in our society. At Vallecitos, they recognize the power and responsibility of all people to be agents of change, and offer an array of innovative retreats and trainings based on the power of awareness, contemplative practice, and experiencing the solitude of the deep woods and wilderness. Change makers are trained in mindfulness, the art of self-knowledge, and critical core competencies of leadership.

Founded in 1993, the Vallecitos Mountain Ranch has been serving the progressive nonprofit communities as a place of refuge. Located high in the Rocky Mountains of northern New Mexico, Vallecitos is a spectacular 135-acre wildlife refuge and mountain sanctuary and the ideal refuge for solitude, quiet, rest, prayer, meditation, healing, reflection and renewal.

The Ranch is located 50 miles west of Taos, New Mexico. The nearest major airport is Albuquerque. Driving time from Albuquerque is 3 1/2 hours; from Santa Fe it is 2 1/2 hours.

To book your retreat, call 575/751.9613, www.vallecitos.org

QUICKIES - HERE'S YOUR BONUS PAGE

- Adrenal Calm cream – for women's adrenals.
- Amberen for menopause support (www.lunadabiomed.com)
- Pomegranate juice – supports men's prostate health.
- Epsom Salt baths – for everyone.
- Maca is a natural Viagra for both men and women.
- NAET for allergy relief.
- My Brain Harmony for children and adults. www.Awokenlife.com
- The Wellness Formula by Source Naturals – for cold and flu-like symptoms.
- Best water on the planet - http://www.pristinehydro.com

WRITE A POSITIVE REVIEW:

www.amazon.com/dp/0979763819 or amazon.com/Forever Young-Ella Croney

- If you like this book ask friends and family to add it to their wish list on Amazon Kindle page and post it on Facebook.
- For a free up to date - Health News Article please email me at info@ellacroney.com your information will not be shared.

WRITE A NEGATIVE REVIEW:

info@ellacroney.com

CHECK OUT MY OTHER BOOK

HEALTHY TIPS ON THE RUN

www.amazon.com/dp/B013HIHZHW

Thanks again

DO'S AND DON'TS

- Do become more aware of Alternative methods of healing.
- Don't try to change your life overnight.
- Do find more time to spend outside in nature.
- Don't buy into quick fix exercise programs.
- Do forgive your past mistakes or perceived failures.
- Don't beat yourself up for what you didn't know, do or can't change. It's all growth.
- Do everything in your power to balance yourself emotionally and mentally.
- Don't give your power to people or situations that create havoc in your life.
- Do start slowly when adding anything new in your daily routine.
- Don't throw conventional medicine out the door. There's room and reason for both Eastern and Western modalities in today's world.

International Natural Healers Association is an amazing resource Center for contacting healers, doctors, teachers all over the world.

Wishing you the happiest, healthiest life you could possibly imagine for now and forever more.

Much luv,
Ella Ladon Croney

ABOUT THE AUTHOR

Ella Croney is a Doctor of Philosophy in Metaphysical Humanistic Science, specializing in Metaphysical Science, Summa Cum Laude. She is a Certified Holistic Life Coach.

Ella loves empowering others with options for rebalancing their lives physically, mentally, emotionally, and spiritually. She knows we all have something to give to the world and this is her gift to you.

Contact her at Ella Croney Productions, 949-436-5006.
Email: info@ellacroney.com
Website: www.ellacroney.com

www.ingramcontent.com/pod-product-compliance
Lightning Source LLC
Chambersburg PA
CBHW070817100426
42742CB00012B/2381